Cambridge Elements

Elements in Indigenous Environmental Research
Series Editors
Dina Gilio-Whitaker
California State University San Marcos
Clint R. Carroll
University of Colorado Boulder
Joy Porter
University of Birmingham
Associate Editor
Matthias Wong
National University of Singapore

INDIGENOUS RIGHTS TO LAND VERSUS EXTRACTIVISM

The Promise and Limits of ILO Convention No. 169 in Mexico

Tamara A. Wattnem
Trinity University

Shaftesbury Road, Cambridge CB2 8EA, United Kingdom

One Liberty Plaza, 20th Floor, New York, NY 10006, USA

477 Williamstown Road, Port Melbourne, VIC 3207, Australia

314–321, 3rd Floor, Plot 3, Splendor Forum, Jasola District Centre, New Delhi – 110025, India

103 Penang Road, #05–06/07, Visioncrest Commercial, Singapore 238467

Cambridge University Press is part of Cambridge University Press & Assessment, a department of the University of Cambridge.

We share the University's mission to contribute to society through the pursuit of education, learning and research at the highest international levels of excellence.

www.cambridge.org
Information on this title: www.cambridge.org/9781009590549

DOI: 10.1017/9781009590532

© Tamara A. Wattnem 2025

This publication is in copyright. Subject to statutory exception and to the provisions of relevant collective licensing agreements, no reproduction of any part may take place without the written permission of Cambridge University Press & Assessment.

When citing this work, please include a reference to the DOI 10.1017/9781009590532

First published 2025

A catalogue record for this publication is available from the British Library

ISBN 978-1-009-59054-9 Hardback
ISBN 978-1-009-59050-1 Paperback
ISSN 2755-0826 (online)
ISSN 2755-0818 (print)

Cambridge University Press & Assessment has no responsibility for the persistence or accuracy of URLs for external or third-party internet websites referred to in this publication and does not guarantee that any content on such websites is, or will remain, accurate or appropriate.

For EU product safety concerns, contact us at Calle de José Abascal, 56, 1°, 28003 Madrid, Spain, or email eugpsr@cambridge.org

Indigenous Rights to Land Versus Extractivism

The Promise and Limits of ILO Convention No. 169 in Mexico

Elements in Indigenous Environmental Research

DOI: 10.1017/9781009590532
First published online: October 2025

Tamara A. Wattnem
Trinity University
Author for correspondence: Tamara A. Wattnem,
tamarawattnem@gmail.com

Abstract: Indigenous and tribal communities often make claims to territory citing their longstanding ties to the land. Since 1989, they increasingly reference ILO Convention No. 169, the only legally binding international agreement on Indigenous and tribal peoples' rights. This Element proposes a three-pronged analytical framework to assess the promise and limits of indigenous rights to land as influenced by international law. The framework calls for the place-specific investigation of the interrelations between: (1) indigenous identity politics, (2) citizenship regimes, and (3) land tenure regimes. Drawing on the case of Mexico, it argues that the ILO Convention has generally been a weak tool for securing rights to ancestral land and for effectively challenging the expansion of extractivism. Still, it has had numerous other significant sociopolitical implications, such as shaping discourses of resistance and incentivizing the use of prior consultation mechanisms in the context of territorial disputes.

Keywords: extractivism, ILO Convention 169, Indigenous peoples' rights, Mexico, land conflicts, ancestral territories

© Tamara A. Wattnem 2025

ISBNs: 9781009590549 (HB), 9781009590501 (PB), 9781009590532 (OC)
ISSNs: 2755-0826 (online), 2755-0818 (print)

Contents

1 Introduction	1
2 Historical Overview and Theoretical Framework	5
3 The Right to Land and Territory in Theory Per ILO Convention No. 169	18
4 Mexico's Formal Engagement with ILO Convention No. 169	22
5 ILO Convention No. 169 in Practice in Mexico	31
6 Conclusion: The Promise and Limits of ILO Convention 169 in Land Disputes	44
References	48

1 Introduction

Indigeneity is increasingly mobilized in the context of land conflicts and movements against the deepening of the extractive frontier, including the expansion of agribusiness, energy industries, infrastructure projects, and mining. It is also used as a frame to argue that certain areas of land, especially territories considered ancestral, should be owned or controlled by Indigenous and tribal communities. Recent high-profile anti-extractive disputes, such as those of the Standing Rock Sioux Tribe in North America, the Sami in Norway, the Lenca communities led by Berta Cáceres in Honduras, and the Waorani in the Ecuadorian Amazon, have placed Indigeneity at the center of movement discourse. In these examples, Indigenous rights over ancestral territories are presented as one of the principal reasons why extractive industries should not be allowed in certain places. In some cases, the demands of Indigenous organizations transcend the specificities of local conflicts and include a broader call to transition to a post-extractive society that centers environmental stewardship and socio-economic justice. Hence, some Indigenous rights movements and organizations have become influential protagonists in the opposition to the regnant accumulation model in the twenty-first century. Better understanding the reach and limitations of ILO Convention 169 in relation to land conflicts allows us to highlight the practical and theoretical dilemmas surrounding the possibility of challenging dominant development paradigms and land use priorities today.

This Element explores the intersection of Indigenous identity politics, claims over ancestral territories, and opposition to the expansion of the extractive frontier, with special attention to the reach and limits of Indigenous rights as established in international law. The International Labor Organization's Indigenous and Tribal Peoples Convention – or ILO Convention No. 169 – is the only legally binding international agreement on Indigenous and tribal peoples rights as of 2025. Convention 169 highlights Indigenous and tribal peoples' right to self-determination and to the territories they have historically inhabited. Since its passing in 1989, it has been repeatedly referenced in the context of land disputes and anti-extractive struggles, most frequently in Latin America. Activists often refer to the Convention as a tool, but what, exactly, has this tool been helpful for with regards to conflicts surrounding land and extractive industries? The objective here is to provide an overview of the material and socio-political implications of the Convention in the context of territorial conflicts thirty years after its ratification, drawing on the case of Mexico to illustrate the central points.

The Mexican example is important because even though it was the second country to ratify ILO Convention 169 (second only to Norway), its material effects in the context of land struggles have been minimal. Understanding why can help us elucidate some of the major limitations of enforcing the Convention after ratification, in both Mexico and elsewhere. Mexico has the largest number of formally recognized Indigenous people in the region, and thus effectively implementing the ideas of the Convention could have momentous consequences. In 2024, the government claimed that there are over seventy different Indigenous groups (*pueblos originarios*) in Mexico. This amounts to over 25 million people who self-identify as Indigenous or Afro-Mexican and is roughly 20 percent of the national population. Despite the high number of Indigenous people, the Mexican case has received noticeably less scholarly attention than other Latin American countries, especially Guatemala, Bolivia, and Peru, where Indigenous populations constitute a higher percentage of the total population and where recent governments have more visibly prioritized the construction of multicultural citizenship regimes. Mexico is also the birthplace of one of the most famous Indigenous rights movements in the world: the EZLN, or Zapatista movement. The EZLN uprising forced the signing of a historic peace agreement with the Mexican government in 1996 – the San Andrés Peace Accords – in which the state agreed to incorporate the principles of ILO Convention 169 into domestic law. Mexico is thus a country that not only signed ILO Convention relatively early, but that also had an armed social movement pressuring the state to act. Lastly, Mexico is one of the most dangerous countries in the world to be an environmental activist, to make claims to land, or to challenge the expansion of the extractive frontier.[1]

Various researchers have drawn attention to the history and politics of Indigenous rights discourses in the context of the broader international human rights movement (Stamatopoulous 1994; Anaya 1996; Rodríguez-Piñero 2005; Larsen and Gilbert 2020), while others have highlighted the gaps between law in theory and law in practice (Chase 2019; Pirsoul 2019). In an important special issue, Larsen and Gilbert (2020) offer a critical perspective on the reach of ILO Convention 169 thirty years after its passing. They suggest that "whereas the international standards recognising Indigenous rights have increased, the gap between these standards, and the aspirations and the realities on the ground remain considerable" (Larsen and Gilbert 2020, 84). This piece builds on their work by drawing attention to the implications of ILO Convention 169 for the

---

[1] As delineated in their 2022 report, Global Witness found that at least 200 land and environmental defenders were killed globally in 2021. Mexico led the list, with fifty-four people killed that year. Most of the assassinations reported were linked to land conflicts involving extractive industries, and over 40 percent of them involved Indigenous people (Global Witness 2022).

politics of land claims and extractivism, highlighting not simply "gaps" between law in theory and in practice, but also what the limits and implications of Convention 169 *as is written* are in relation to territorial disputes.

The starting point is to acknowledge the inherently paradoxical nature of the global human rights regime, which on the one hand relies on claims to universality and individual as opposed to collective rights, but on the other, is deeply shaped and constrained by local-level politics, enforcement challenges, power relations, and competing interpretations. For Stern and Straus (2014), "this contradiction always structures human rights. There can be no human rights without a claim to the universal, to the transnational, and to transcendent principles. But there can also be no human rights without locality, politics, history, and actors" (p. 9). Indigenous and tribal peoples' rights have the added tension of being collective and minority rights – applying solely to a subset of humanity as opposed to humanity as a whole – and hence face greater legitimacy and enforcement challenges at the local level. Grounded contextual analysis is crucial for revealing how the global Indigenous rights framework plays out in practice.

The proposed framework for studying the place-specific implications of the intersection between Indigenous identities and land conflicts is to investigate the dynamic interrelations between the following three variables:

1. *The local construction of Indigenous and tribal identities:* A historical analysis of the local and national level politics surrounding the construction of Indigenous and tribal identities, their political relevance, ongoing disputes over who truly counts as an Indigenous or tribal person, and how these changes are institutionalized by the state over time.
2. *Citizenship regimes:* An analysis of the historically specific features of citizenship regimes and the changing configurations of rights and obligations that exist in a specific time and place, with special attention to the conditions under which Indigenous and/or tribal populations can claim "special" rights, to land or otherwise.
3. *Land tenure regimes:* The place-specific forms of land tenure that exist, including land use priorities as established by the state, the legal status of extractive industries, land ownership patterns, and the existence of formally recognized collective forms of land tenure (particularly those that recognize and delimit Indigenous territories) and their interrelations with citizenship regimes.

The logic is that investigating the characteristics and interactions (or lack thereof) between these three variables can help us better understand the material, socio-political, and ideological implications of Indigenous identity politics in relation to land struggles in different places. Together, they point to the subjective, political, and economic dynamics that shape and constrain the local level defense of Indigenous and tribal peoples' rights to land. They bridge the local and the global in a way that acknowledges their co-constitution but that is also attentive to place-based historical specificity. They also provide an analytical compass for cross-national comparative historical research. Local and national level processes need to be thought of as embedded in a global political economy, pressured by powerful domestic and transnational extractive and agrarian elites, and influenced by an international human rights framework that increasingly calls for the protection of minority rights. This is a minimalist framework and will likely benefit from attention to additional themes as relevant in specific times and places.

I argue that even though ILO Convention 169 is often mobilized in the context of land disputes, it has not been a particularly effective tool for securing rights to ancestral land nor for vetoing or reversing the expansion of extractive industries. In fact, it has had minimal direct material implications vis-à-vis extractivism. Nonetheless, the ideas in the Convention have had numerous other sociopolitical implications that are significant and place specific. At the most abstract level, the Convention has provided a language for claiming rights that is promoted and legitimated by the international human rights regime. More practically, it has encouraged the call for "prior consultations" in the context of land conflicts and has turned procedures that seek to demonstrate "free, prior and informed consent" (FPIC) into the key mechanism of conflict resolution. Per the Convention, disputes over extractivism, or over any other matter affecting Indigenous and tribal peoples, are to be addressed via consultations and the achievement of FPIC. This has incentivized transforming conflicts over land and the political economy of extractivism into local issues and provoked heated debates regarding who is entitled to organize and participate in prior consultations and who is not. This is closely related to the delicate question of who *really* is Indigenous and, consequently, deserving of "special" rights. Because identity politics is at the center of the conversation, other crucial questions about the power of capital, class tensions, unequal power relations within and across rural communities, and the role of the state in prioritizing extractivism are sidelined. Moreover, the outcomes of prior consultations are not binding, so they can become instruments of a sort of dispossession with consultation. This is not to deny that many communities and organizations do consider the Convention a valuable tool for the defense of various rights, independent of its practical limitations in relation to territorial conflicts.

The rest of the text is organized as follows. It first provides a brief historical contextualization of the emergence of Indigenous and tribal peoples' rights at the global level. It then frames the argument in relation to literature about the role of Indigeneity in neoliberal citizenship regimes and the rapid expansion of extractive industries in the late twentieth and early twenty-first centuries. The introductory section details the logic behind the three-pronged framework introduced above, which will then be used to discuss the Mexican case in more detail. The second half of the Element addresses the content of ILO Convention 169 in relation to territorial disputes, with particular attention to how it has been used in Mexico. It addresses two major questions: (1) What role has ILO Convention No. 169 played in the context of territorial disputes in Mexico? (2) How can we best study the material and socio-political implications of Indigenous rights as established in international law in relation to land conflicts beyond Mexico, especially those that involve extractive industries?

The main primary sources analyzed are Convention No. 169 itself and all the documents pertaining to Mexico's application of the Convention produced by the ILO's supervisory system, which monitors progress or lack thereof in different countries that have ratified Conventions.[2] These sources allow us to understand how Mexican organizations and state officials have engaged with the ideas that are part of ILO Convention 169 and illustrate how the ILO responds to allegations of the inappropriate compliance of its conventions. I also rely on media and reports about cases in which Indigenous politics and anti-extractive struggles intersect, two interviews with high-ranking public servants working within Mexico's Energy Ministry, and archival research related to Mexico's energy and mining political economy since the 1980s. Altogether, the Element shows why the ratification of ILO Convention 169 in Mexico has had such limited material implications in the context of territorial disputes, and in the process, presents an analytical framework through which to investigate the intersection of Indigenous politics and land conflicts elsewhere in the world.

2 Historical Overview and Theoretical Framework

The reach and limits of ILO Convention 169 in relation to land conflicts and extractive industries can be best understood by considering the interrelations between: (a) ongoing disputes over definitions of Indigeneity and related trends in the international Indigenous rights regime; (b) the particularities of regnant citizenship regimes; and (c) the politics of land tenure regimes in the context of the rapid expansion of extractivism during the late twentieth and early twenty-first centuries. This section addresses these three themes in historical

---

[2] These sources are public and can be found on the ILO website.

perspective prior to discussing the specificities of the role of ILO Convention No. 169 in relation to land struggles in Mexico.

Indigeneity and Indigenous Peoples' Rights in Historical Perspective

Indigenous peoples' rights at the global level are governed by the International Labor Organization (ILO). The ILO was founded in 1919 by the League of Nations to address labor issues in the aftermath of World War I, and it later became a specialized agency of the United Nations. Throughout the first half of the twentieth century, one of its key concerns was the colonial era distinction between citizens and Indigenous laborers, as it sought to introduce labor standards meant to improve the subpar labor conditions and exploitation of "native" and "colored" people that predominated during colonial times (Rodríguez-Piñero 2005). The thematic focus was on establishing rules and standards around forced labor, recruitment processes, and employment contracts. Early ILO conventions dealing with "native" workers were not separate from those focusing on "rural workers" more generally, as the assumption was that many Indigenous and tribal people were rural workers too, and hence appropriately covered by those Conventions. In this way, early ILO Conventions pertinent to Indigenous and tribal peoples were intimately tied to debates about citizenship and labor regimes institutionalized during colonial times.

In the context of the mid-twentieth-century decolonization wave, ILO delegates began to think about issues affecting Indigenous peoples differently, beyond the narrow lens of labor rights. This shift was reflected in a 1953 publication titled "Indigenous peoples: Living and working conditions of aboriginal populations in independent countries," in which the ILO argued that Indigenous peoples needed to be the subject of special and targeted public policies to improve their living standards, as opposed to assuming that they were sufficiently covered via existing ILO conventions (ILO 2019). In this spirit, in 1957, the ILO adopted Convention No. 107, the first international convention dealing specifically with Indigenous and tribal populations, still in force in seventeen countries.[3] Unlike prior conventions, C107 went well beyond addressing labor rights, and instead called for the need to guarantee appropriate

---

[3] Twenty-seven countries ratified ILO Convention No. 107, namely: Angola, Argentina, Bangladesh, Belgium, Bolivia, Brazil, Colombia, Costa Rica, Cuba, Dominican Republic, Ecuador, Egypt, El Salvador, Ghana, Guinea-Bissau, Haiti, India, Iraq, Malawi, Mexico, Pakistan, Panama, Paraguay, Peru, Portugal, Syria and Tunisia. It is no longer in force in 10 of these (Argentina, Bolivia, Brazil, Colombia, Costa Rica, Ecuador, Mexico, Paraguay, Peru, and Portugal), as they have ratified Convention No. 169 as a replacement.

education and health services for Indigenous populations, as well as the general need for their "economic improvement." It also drew attention to the special link between Indigenous communities and land, a relationship that continues to be at the core of contemporary Indigenous rights demands. The language was unapologetically assimilationist and sought to "integrate" Indigenous peoples into the broader society. Despite its limitations and biases as seen through contemporary eyes, the 1957 Convention laid the groundwork for incorporating Indigenous peoples' rights into the broader international human rights framework (Anaya 1996). In short, the ILO has played a major role in the early drafting of international legal standards concerning Indigenous peoples and, relatedly, defining what it means to be Indigenous in the first place (Rodríguez-Piñero 2005).

Legal and philosophical discussions about natives, aboriginals, and Indigenous peoples, of course, predate the ILO. These conversations emerged with and were fundamental to colonial and imperial projects. Debates surrounding Latin American colonization were crucial for the development of international law in relation to Indigenous peoples. As early as the sixteenth century, political theorists and missionaries – perhaps most famously Fray Bartolomé de las Casas – denounced the brutality of the Spanish colonial project and the dispossession that accompanied it. A heated debate ensued regarding the legality of territorial dispossession, the humanity of Indigenous peoples, and the legitimacy of empire. These colonial-era discussions directly influenced the early features of modern international law as related to Indigeneity (Anaya 1996).

Increasingly vibrant local and transnational Indigenous peoples' rights movements gained traction beginning in the 1960s, with organizations from the Americas playing a particularly influential leadership role. By the 1980s, the ILO's assimilationist approach was increasingly condemned, and numerous voices called for a revision of Convention No. 107. After many long and polarizing debates, ILO Convention No. 169 was passed in 1989, and it continues to be the regnant international convention on Indigenous and tribal peoples' rights. Whereas C107 prioritized assimilation and integration, C169 highlights the value of difference, autonomy, self-determination, and cultural rights. Norway was the first country to ratify it in June 1990, followed by Mexico in September 1990. As of 2025, the twenty-four countries colored in the map below had ratified Convention No. 169,[4] making it one of the least ratified ILO Conventions in the world (Figure 1).

---

[4] The countries that have ratified ILO Convention No. 169 as of 2023 are: Argentina, Bolivia, Brazil, Central African Republic, Chile, Colombia, Costa Rica, Denmark, Dominica, Ecuador,

Figure 1 Countries that have ratified ILO Convention No. 169 as of 2024. Credit: created with mapchart.net.

Fifteen out of the twenty-four countries that have ratified the Convention are in Latin America and the Caribbean. There are other important global initiatives that also address Indigenous peoples' rights, including the Permanent Forum on Indigenous Issues (PFII), the UN Voluntary Fund for Indigenous Peoples, and the 1996 UN Declaration on the Rights of Indigenous Peoples (UNDRIP). The critical difference is that only ILO Convention No. 169 is legally binding.

The ILO holds an annual conference – the International Labour Conference – attended by representatives of state, labor, and employer organizations from across the world. Given the ILO's institutional history and its tripartite structure (with labor, business, and state actors having a seat at the table), Indigenous rights struggles are institutionally intertwined with labor politics. Paradoxically, while the Convention advocates for the systematic participation of Indigenous peoples in all matters affecting them, there are no formal mechanisms for Indigenous people to directly engage with the ILO (Larsen 2020). The key communication channels between different countries and the ILO are worker organizations, employer organizations, and states, all of which many Indigenous communities are weakly represented by, if at all. During the 1988 and 1989 sessions, when the content of ILO Convention 169 was under discussion, "Special arrangements were made to allow representatives of indigenous groups limited participation in the deliberations of the conference committee

---

Fiji, Germany, Guatemala, Honduras, Luxemburg, Mexico, Nepal, Netherlands, Nicaragua, Norway, Paraguay, Peru, Spain, and Venezuela.

designated for the revision" (Anaya 1996, 47). Still, there isn't an adequate institutional mechanism for Indigenous and tribal communities to communicate concerns directly to the ILO. Larsen (2020) has described this as generating a "cuckoo effect," insofar "it entails indigenous organisations relying on the nesting, reporting, and filing of representations by others, much like to cuckoos rely on the 'parasitic' nesting by other birds" (p. 104). Thus, there tends to be a significant "disconnect between country delegations and indigenous policy priorities" (Larsen 2020, 103).

ILO Convention No. 169 is premised on two major assumptions: (1) that its definition of Indigeneity holds globally; and (2) that Indigenous and tribal peoples have universal and special collective rights that should be adopted in every country's domestic legal framework. Critically, it contains the only legally binding definition of Indigenous and tribal peoples that aspires to be universal. Merely at that level, it is a document with a controversial and by no means neutral argument of global significance. Article 1.2 of the Convention states: "Self-identification as indigenous or tribal shall be regarded as a fundamental criterion for determining the groups to which the provisions of this Convention apply." Self-identification, however, has not historically been the metric whereby states define Indigeneity and tribal populations. In fact, in some countries, both state authorities and locals have challenged the relevance of Indigeneity as a politically salient and locally relevant identity category. Delegates to the ILO from various African countries, the USSR, India, and China, for example, previously argued that they didn't truly have Indigenous people, but rather only minorities and tribal populations. The question of Indigeneity, they claimed, was primarily relevant in Latin America. Even some Latin American politicians formerly denied the socio-political relevance of Indigeneity and instead highlighted the systematic mixing of all races (*mestizaje*). This is beginning to change, in part because the criterion of self-identification has contributed to making the language of Indigeneity increasingly meaningful in places where it was once relatively uninfluential. Thus, C169 is a significant document even in contexts in which it has not been ratified or where Indigeneity has not hitherto been a particularly salient identity category for domestic politics. Still, the fact that most countries have not ratified the Convention signals how sensitive and polarizing the ideas it espouses can be.

C169 glosses over the complex processes whereby people come to speak of themselves as Indigenous or not. Anthropologists and sociologists have long drawn attention to the socially constructed, fluid, and historically contingent features of identities and cultures. Indigeneity is anything but a static or self-evident identity category. State-sanctioned definitions of Indigeneity vary across time and place, as well as the conditions under which people come to describe themselves as Indigenous, and thus we cannot assume a fixed ahistorical Indigeneity. Competing definitions have differing views and assumptions about the legacies of imperialism, internal/domestic colonialism, the displacement that has accompanied the expansion of capitalist political economy, and importantly, how one could go about remedying this history of violence and dispossession.

There is important recent scholarship tracing the multiple ways in which Indigeneity is being deployed, contested, redefined, and even abused in various contexts. Haley (2024), for example, is interested in neo-Indigenism as "a global social phenomenon that has arisen over the past half-century. It features assertions of indigenous identity by persons lacking indigenous ancestries, histories, or social ties. In the Western hemisphere, it is neo-Indianism, with variants asserting specific identities" (Haley 2024, 1). In a similar spirit, Galinier and Molinié's (2013) work traces the ethnogenesis of "neo-Indians" in Latin America since the 1970s, especially in Mexico and Peru. For them, the neo-Indian phenomenon is intrinsically tied to contemporary globalization. They depict them as follows:

> The "neo-Indians" gradually emerging in the New World are neither the archetypes of ethnographic monographs nor the mixed-race creations of antiracist intellectuals; they are closer to our Disneyland culture. In their day-to-day lives, they wear polyester rather than feathers, although they dress as Aztec princes or Incas for celebrations, wearing traditional clothing that could inspire Californian designers. Instead of attracting rain, their dances are now geared toward attracting tourists, even if, at times, in their shantytown hovels, they improvise salsas with an indigenous vein. They are sometimes active in Indianist movements invoking an identity that, in reality, is no longer theirs. In any event, they offer themselves to elites who do not hesitate to appropriate their cast-off clothes and to indigenous communities whose traditional culture is in shreds, as well as to nations in search of autochthony. Indians used to pay material tribute to the Spanish throne—now they pay with their image, although they style their looks as they see fit (Galinier and Molinié 2013, viii).

Implicit in their argument is a distinction between this novel expression of "neo-Indians" vs. other, more "authentic" or "real" Indians that escape this portrayal. These complex and sensitive disputes over authenticity at the local level are rendered secondary and unimportant by C169 insofar as it foregrounds self-identification as the metric by which to determine Indigenous identities.

Other researchers have identified cases where people are accused of falsely or even fraudulently claiming to be Indigenous. Haley and Wilcoxon's (2005) study of the ethnogenesis of the neo-Chumash identity in California is instructive in this regard. Neo-Chumash identity first emerged in the late 1960s and

1970s, but unlike other local Indigenous groups, they "lack Chumash or other Native Californian ancestry and are descended almost exclusively from the people who colonized California for Spain from 1769 to 1820" (Haley and Wilcoxon 2005, 432). Thus, "It is tempting to suggest that neo-Chumash are perpetrating 'ethnic fraud' by asserting ancestry they do not have" (Haley and Wilcoxon 2005, 432). But the authors suggest that this is not necessarily the best way to think about it, especially if one takes a comparative historical perspective and considers multiple other examples of malleable and continuously reformulated identities, both Indigenous and not. Their point is that it is not rare for identities and cultural memories to be reinvented and reframed in response to changing contexts and challenges. Haley and Wilcoxon's (2005) historical research shows how neo-Chumash identity emerged "as an identity lost salience amidst changing conditions, as subjects sought higher status, or because of a combination of these" (p. 441). This fluidity, they suggest, is not unique to the neo-Chumash, and thus authenticity is relative and context specific. Indigeneity is therefore never a primordial and ahistorical identity of self-described Indigenous peoples that remains static across generations.

This is not to suggest that in certain contexts the self-ascription of Indigenous identities cannot have pernicious effects in the context of disputes over land and resources. Literature on "pretendianism," or false claims to Indigenous ancestry, has grown in the US and Canada. Leroux's (2019, 2024) research in Quebec, for example, highlights the problems that can arise from "wrongful" claims to Indigeneity when they are levied to claim territory, especially against other groups with clearer, and perhaps more legitimate, historical ties to land. Leroux (2019) examines "a social phenomenon that has been in full flight since the turn of the twenty-first century: the shifting of otherwise white, French descendants in Canada (and the United States) into an Indigenous identity" (p. 1). He focuses on cases whereby French descendants use an "Indigenous ancestor born between 300 and 375 years ago as the basis for a contemporary 'Indigenous' identity" (p. 2). For Leroux (2019), this "race-shifting" "consolidates contemporary forms of colonialism that oppose actual Indigenous peoples in the present" (p. 214).

Communities that mobilize Indigeneity today make place with reference to colonial history and legacies. Indigeneity becomes politically relevant in relation to contemporary narratives retelling colonial and post-colonial history. These stories can have real border-making and political implications. They also have consequences for the ability to claim "special" collective rights. Pre-colonial migration dynamics, especially those not directly related to European modernity, tend to be comparatively less visible and even deemed irrelevant to contemporary understandings of Indigeneity. Power relations and tensions between and within Indigenous populations themselves are also of secondary importance. Ultimately, it is a battle over narratives and historical interpretations with direct implications for contemporary claims to land, territory, and rights. Now that Indigeneity is at times associated with the ability to claim "special" rights, a growing number of people are proudly adopting that identity, making the politics of self-identification particularly controversial. For all these reasons, the history and politics surrounding official definitions of Indigeneity are crucial variables that need to be understood when thinking about the intersection of Indigenous identity politics and territorial disputes.

Citizenship Regimes and Indigenous Peoples' Rights

This section addresses the relationship between citizenship regimes and Indigenous peoples' rights, sometimes institutionalized as multicultural citizenship regimes. It is crucial to study the features of prevailing citizenship regimes when trying to understand the reach and limits of ILO Convention No. 169 in practice, especially whether "special" rights are granted based on self-identification as Indigenous, and if so, what those rights are. I draw on Yashar's understanding of "citizenship regimes," that is, the historically contingent "differentiated bundle of rights and responsibilities that can include civil rights (freedom of organization and expression), political rights (suffrage), and social rights (the right to a minimum standard of living)" (Yashar 1999, 79). I pay particular attention to the recent establishment of multicultural citizenship regimes across Latin America.

The strengthening of both domestic and transnational Indigenous rights frameworks coincided with the introduction of neoliberal policies in much of the world. Following Harvey, I understand neoliberalization as both a political project for the restoration of class power and "a theory of political economic practices that proposes that human well-being can best be advanced by liberating individual entrepreneurial freedoms and skills within an institutional framework characterized by strong private property rights, free markets, and free trade" (Harvey 2005, 2). Counterintuitively, while neoliberal theory exhorts the individual and individual rights, the political salience of identity-based collective rights increased as part of neoliberal reform processes. In Latin America, multicultural citizenship regimes were adopted in the context of the deepening of neoliberal reforms, and hence new rights were recognized while numerous public services and subsidies were eroded. In other words, new cultural rights were recognized while previously protected ones, especially social and economic rights, were weakened. The simultaneous adoption of neoliberal policies alongside demands for greater autonomy, local participation, and recognition of cultural rights has led scholars to speak of "neoliberal multiculturalism" (Hale 2002; Speed and Sierra 2005).

Human rights and multiculturalism are the most commonly used frames in discussions about Indigenous peoples' rights in Latin America. The politics behind the establishment of multicultural citizenship regimes vary across the region, but in all cases, it was a socio-political novelty. Even though debates surrounding ethno-racial classification have long been an important part of Latin American politics, it was not long ago that Latin American states denied the political and cultural relevance of Indigeneity as a state-sanctioned identity category deserving of special rights. As Loveman (2014) notes,

> Latin American national myths long celebrated the idea that distinctive peoples were formed through the mixture of races and thus dissolution of racial differences. As a corollary to these national myths, many Latin American states declared themselves officially colorblind, actively discouraged individual racial identification, and highlighted the supposed absence of racial divisions or discrimination within their nations (Loveman 2014, xii).

Prior to neoliberalization, in line with the assimilationist and integrationist outlook that dominated at the time, Latin American states generally sought to sideline the political relevance of ethnic identities, fomented nationalism, and categorized Indians as peasants or workers. The idea was to incentivize the adoption of a class identity by Indians, and this became a structural feature of the corporatist project in many Latin American countries. This began to change alongside the introduction of neoliberal policies, and in response to the rise of social movements that placed Indigenous identity at the center of people's demands. By the 1990s, Indigenous rights movements were "most prominent in countries with large and moderate-size indigenous populations (Bolivia, Guatemala, Ecuador, and Mexico), but they have also provoked important debates and reforms in countries with small indigenous populations (Colombia, Brazil, and Chile)" (Yashar 1999, 77). These movements articulated "ethnic-based agendas that contest the definition and terms of national citizenship, both insisting on greater inclusion in the national state and greater autonomy from it" (Yashar 2007, 174).

Multicultural models of citizenship do not assume a culturally homogeneous population and establish differentiated rights for certain populations. Many Latin American countries introduced changes to their Constitutions and laws in the 1990s and early 2000s that recognized special rights for ethnic and racial minorities (Fontana and Grugel 2016). In the spirit of ILO Convention 169, domestic Indigenous rights frameworks allegedly seek to protect cultural integrity, grant some degree of autonomy, and foment participatory engagement. The logic is "that indigenous peoples are entitled to be different but are not necessarily to be considered a priori unconnected from larger social and political structures" (Anaya 2004, 60). This represented a "clear shift in the official stance of most governments away from the ideal of color-blind integration. In lieu of celebrating mestizaje, a growing number of Latin American countries now celebrate multiethnicity" (Loveman 2014, 269). In the aftermath of the recognition of Indigenous peoples' rights and the associated right to have special rights, there is an ongoing debate regarding which specific unique rights and arrangements are to be permitted, which are not, and why. The implementation of the ideas of ILO Convention No. 169 is one aspect of this broader debate.

The argument for Indigenous rights, or minority rights more broadly, is often framed as an argument in defense of cultural rights. The demand for cultural rights, by definition a collective endeavor, is at odds with individualistic understandings of human rights and citizenship. For Yashar (2005), multicultural citizenship regimes represent a "postliberal challenge," insofar as different or special rights are demanded based on collective identities. To complicate matters further, Indigenous peoples' cultural rights are construed such that they have an inextricable material component linked to territorial rights, the logic being that the reproduction of Indigenous culture is dependent on people's longstanding ties to specific territories. The debates surrounding the implications of collective rights vs. individual rights inevitably lead to a tense debate over boundary making, closely tied to the politics of self-identification as Indigenous and the political and material implications of that.

Three of the particularly challenging questions that are part of these debates include: Why should Indigenous and tribal peoples have rights that other oppressed or discriminated populations do not, especially land? Who is "authentically" Indigenous and/or tribal, and who gets to determine that? How can one objectively determine the boundaries of "traditional" Indigenous territories after so many waves of displacement, colonization, and migration? These complex questions are at the core of the delicate politics of the adoption and mobilization of ILO Convention 169 at the local level. The outcome of these debates determines who is to have the right to have "special" rights, including the right to prior consultation over land use and ownership. Paying attention to the specificities of multicultural citizenship regimes, especially in relation to the ability to effectively make claims to land based on Indigeneity, is crucial for understanding the promise and limits of ILO Convention No. 169 in the face of territorial disputes. This theme will be revisited later in the text in relation to Mexico, but is of relevance in any context in which Indigeneity is being mobilized to make claims to land.

Land Tenure Regimes and the Prioritization of Extractivism

The ability of Indigenous and tribal peoples to successfully make claims to land partially depends on the existence of a land tenure regime that formally recognizes and safeguards their rights to ancestral territories, and/or that provides avenues for groups to demand land based on Indigeneity. The state-sanctioned recognition of Indigenous and tribal territories varies widely across countries, with some countries having legally defined and enforced land tenure options for Indigenous groups while others do not. The third element of the analytical framework, therefore, calls for an understanding of regnant land tenure regimes, particularly whether they facilitate or obstruct the official recognition and protection of land based on Indigenous or tribal identities. For example, as will be addressed in more detail later, the prioritization of hydrocarbon extraction and mining over any other land use in Mexico in the name of the "national interest" is one of the major obstacles to the effective recognition of Indigenous rights to territory. In Mexico, the laws are such that the power of extractive industries tends to override claims to land based on Indigeneity. Thus, it is crucial to consider the intersection of the "postliberal challenge" with the politics of domestic land regimes, in the face of pressures from evermore powerful extractive industries, both domestic and transnational.

In Latin America, the institutionalization of multicultural citizenship regimes coincided with the rapid expansion of extractive industries. The reigning accumulation logic depends on the systematic extraction of evermore natural resources and thus the deepening of the extractive frontier to areas once considered unproductive, creating new socio-environmental conflicts, or exacerbating pre-existing ones (Temper et al. 2015). The early twenty-first century has been variously referred to by influential Latin American theorists as an age of neo-extractivism (Gudynas 2015), of the "commodities consensus" (Svampa 2015), and/or reprimarization of the economy, that is, a renewed dependence on the export of primary materials. Extractivism and the "commodities consensus" refer to a development model "based on the large-scale exportation of raw materials, such as hydrocarbons (gas and petroleum), metals and minerals (copper, gold, silver, tin, bauxite, zinc, etc.), agricultural products (corn, soy, and wheat), and biofuels" (Svampa 2015, 65). The term "consensus" implies that there is a political-ideological aspect regarding the desirability of extractivism, oftentimes framed as a comparative advantage. Neo-extractivism, in turn, refers to the deepening of extractivism with a social justice redistributive agenda (Burchardt and Dietz 2014; Gudynas 2015).

The term "neo-extractivism" is usually used to refer to countries that were part of the "left turn" or "pink tide" during the early twenty-first century in South America. Overlapping with the electoral ascendancy of the Left, between 2000 and 2014, demand from China drove historically high global commodity prices. This made exporting commodities particularly seductive and profitable. Pink tide governments used revenue generated by extractive industries for redistribution purposes and social programs as opposed to solely for private profit. These administrations questioned orthodox neoliberalism without challenging the primacy of extractivism as a central element of the countries' political economy and generally maintained their associations with transnational capital. The growing demand for minerals and natural resources, driven in part by rising demand from China and other BRICS countries during the first decade of the twenty-first century, led to an intensification of disputes around land use.

State actors that promote the desirability of extractive industries often frame any alternative development logic as unreasonable and disadvantageous (Bebbington and Bury 2013). Opposition to extractivism is even "considered in terms of antimodernity, negating progress, 'infantile ecologism,' or even 'colonial environmentalism'" (Svampa 2015, 67). Gudynas (2016) goes so far as to suggest that the current prioritization of extractivism has a theological aspect in that arguments promoting it are akin to a religious belief system. Riofrancos (2020) makes a useful analytical distinction between two different types of resource radicalisms that characterize contemporary Latin American politics, namely: (1) *resource nationalism*, demanding collective ownership of oil and minerals in the name of social justice and redistribution; and (2) *anti-extractivism*, which rejects the centrality of extractive industries and envisions a transition to a post-extractive world. What exactly a post-extractive society would look like is less clear and is the subject of ongoing debates (Riofrancos 2020).

Numerous researchers have studied the connection between extraction of non-renewable resources, enclosures, and accumulation by dispossession (Borras et al. 2011; Sassen 2013; Bebbington and Bury 2013). Connected to studies of enclosure and dispossession are also dozens of studies of grassroots resistance to the expansion of the reigning extractivist development model (Peet and Watts 2004; Veltmeyer and Petras 2014). The proliferation of anti-extractive movements that foreground demands over territory and the environment is sometimes described as indicative of an "ecoterritorial turn" in social movement scholarship. The ecoterritorial turn points to social-environmental struggles in which communitarian, Indigenous, and environmental discourses intersect, oftentimes in relation to a critique of extractivism. These struggles push us to question what is considered development to begin with and what sorts of economic activities should be prioritized and valued.

As the extractive frontier has grown, violence against environmental activists has intensified. In 2017 alone, 197 "land and environment defenders" were killed across the globe (IWGIA 2018). Some 60 percent of these murders occurred in Latin America, making it the world's deadliest region for activists resisting mining, oil, agribusiness, and similar projects. By November 2023, EJAtlas reported 3,879 environmental conflicts worldwide, many of which involve extractive industries. The five countries with the highest number of reported conflicts are: (1) India, 395 conflicts; (2) USA, 386 conflicts; (3) Mexico, 279 conflicts; (4) China, 251 conflicts; and (5) Brazil, 220 conflicts. These are not exhaustive numbers as they rely on people voluntarily reporting conflicts, and so there are undoubtedly many more unreported conflicts globally. What is clear is that a critique of the prioritization of extractive industries as an essential part of the regnant development model is a cross-cutting theme in socio-environmental conflicts worldwide.

Territorial disputes and conflicts surrounding the expansion of the extractive frontier are by no means solely Indigenous or rural issues, nor are all Indigenous organizations actively part of anti-extractive struggles. There is immense variation regarding the nature and motivations of opposition to extractive industries by Indigenous and non-Indigenous communities. Some are organizing against state-run extractive projects, others against domestic private corporations, and still others against transnational investors. Oftentimes, communities are divided in terms of the perceived pros and cons of allowing extractive industries to operate in their areas. Importantly, many people support them given the employment opportunities they provide and the income they sometimes generate for both local and national governments. Indigenous and tribal peoples are evidently not a unified block against extractive industries. Still, unlike other segments of the world's population, Indigenous and tribal communities can mobilize international law as part of territorial and environmental justice disputes. In so doing, they are shaping contemporary collective action frames, discourses, and strategies of resistance, sidelining other potential frames under which to make claims to land or to challenge the centrality and power of extractive industries in today's global political economy. Prior to discussing additional details of the Mexican case, the next section addresses the formal wording of ILO Convention No. 169 with regard to rights to land and territory.

3 The Right to Land and Territory in Theory Per ILO Convention No. 169

ILO Convention No. 169 upholds Indigenous and tribal peoples' right to the land they have historically inhabited. If this idea translated into actual policy and systematic land titling processes, it would have far-reaching implications in land tenure regimes worldwide. Unsurprisingly, then, the sections of the Convention upholding Indigenous and tribal peoples' rights to land were particularly polarizing throughout the negotiation process that anteceded its approval in the 1980s. Disagreements with these ideas are reflected in the comparatively low ratification numbers of the Convention. This section provides an overview of the formal wording of ILO Convention 169 with regard to rights over land and territory *in theory*, prior to discussing how the Convention has played out *in practice* in Mexico.

C169 is composed of a preamble and forty-four articles, divided into ten parts. Part I addresses matters of general policy, whereas Part II discusses issues directly related to land (articles 13 through 19). The general policy segment introduces the idea that Indigenous and tribal peoples have the right to decide their own development priorities "to the extent possible" and to participate in all matters which may affect them directly. In Part II, Article 14 establishes that "The rights of ownership and possession of the peoples concerned over the lands which they traditionally occupy shall be recognized." This is the article that is most frequently referenced in the context of struggles that rely on the Convention's language to legitimize claims to territory. Article 13.2 specifies that the use of the term "land" includes "the concept of territories, which covers the total environment of the areas which the peoples concerned occupy or otherwise use." Article 15.1 goes on to state that "The rights of the peoples concerned to the natural resources pertaining to their lands shall be specially safeguarded. These rights include the right of these peoples to participate in the use, management and conservation of these resources." In practice, the issue of delimiting and protecting ancestral land under *traditional* occupation is immensely complicated in a post-colonial world that has undergone multiple waves of displacement and dispossession.

The component of ILO Convention 169 that has received the most attention in policy circles is the right it grants to Indigenous and tribal peoples to participate directly in all matters that affect them. Participation became a buzzword in the context of neoliberal globalization and was systematically discussed by the mainstream development establishment as an unproblematic virtue (Leal 2007). The participation mechanism the

Convention promotes is that of prior consultations, with the alleged objective of obtaining "free, prior and informed consent" (FPIC) before any policy or project that affects Indigenous lands and livelihoods goes into effect. The organization and governance of prior consultations have become the central policy instrument for the implementation of Convention 169 at the local level. Article 6.1 lays out the spirit that should supposedly guide the organization of prior consultations. It states:

> Governments shall: (a) consult the peoples concerned, through appropriate procedures and in particular through their representative institutions, whenever consideration is being given to legislative or administrative measures which may affect them directly; (b) establish means by which these peoples can freely participate, to at least the same extent as other sectors of the population, at all levels of decision-making in elective institutions and administrative and other bodies responsible for policies and programmes which concern them; (c) establish means for the full development of these peoples' own institutions and initiatives, and in appropriate cases provide the resources necessary for this purpose (ILO Convention 169, Article 6.1).

Article 6.2 adds: "The consultations carried out in application of this Convention shall be undertaken, in good faith and in a form appropriate to the circumstances, with the objective of achieving agreement or consent to the proposed measures." The final phrase merits repetition: *with the objective of achieving agreement or consent to the proposed measures.* In other words, prior consultations are intended to be consent-producing mechanisms, rather than tools to defend territory and land. Per the Convention's phrasing, there is no recognized option for outright rejecting a policy, program, or concession for extractivism to which a particular community may be opposed.

In many Latin American countries, debates surrounding the logistics of organizing prior consultations have been at the center of the conversation regarding the implementation of C169, both from the point of view of grassroots actors and state officials. Major practical challenges and dilemmas have arisen from these debates. For example, what exactly are "appropriate procedures," who decides, and how can we know when procedures are inappropriate? What are legitimate "representative institutions" and from whose point of view? More fundamentally, who decides who *really* is Indigenous and hence deserving of the right to prior consultation? For Fontana and Grugel (2016), "FPIC offers partial redress for profound, historical marginalization; but in so doing it embeds a potentially powerful exclusionary ontology and runs the risk of violating the notion of equal national citizenship" (p. 256).

Articles 15, 16, and 17 touch on additional matters that are vital for the political economy of extractive industries, especially for the possibility of legally justifying displacement and dispossession. Article 15.2, for example, states:

> In cases in which the State retains the ownership of mineral or sub-surface resources or rights to other resources pertaining to lands, governments shall establish or maintain procedures through which they shall consult these peoples, with a view to ascertaining whether and to what degree their interests would be prejudiced, before undertaking or permitting any programmes for the exploration or exploitation of such resources pertaining to their lands. The people concerned shall, wherever possible, participate in the benefits of such activities and shall receive fair compensation for any damages which they may sustain as a result of such activities.

Article 16.2 adds:

> Where the relocation of these peoples is considered necessary as an exceptional measure, such relocation shall take place only with their free and informed consent. Where their consent cannot be obtained, such relocation shall take place only following appropriate procedures established by national laws and regulations, including public inquiries where appropriate, which provide the opportunity for effective representation of the peoples concerned.

Reiterating the primacy of prior consultations as a technology of government to deal with conflicts over land, Article 17.2 suggests: "The peoples concerned shall be consulted whenever consideration is being given to their capacity to alienate their lands or otherwise transmit their rights outside their own community." In short, even though Indigenous and tribal peoples allegedly have the right to determine the "development priorities" in their traditional lands, they have no real enforceable rights to veto activities they may consider undesirable. The Convention therefore allows for displacement and dispossession, but with the bonus of participation, and in some cases, compensation, and benefit sharing. Still, numerous Indigenous communities have defended their right to prior consultation, despite its limitations in practice.

Many Latin American nations incorporated prior consultations into their Constitutions (including Bolivia, Colombia, Ecuador, Guatemala, Paraguay, and Peru), while others incorporated them into laws regulating certain industries, especially mining and hydrocarbon extraction (ILO 2019). The Bolivian and Peruvian states have been particularly proactive in designing and attempting to implement rules and regulations on prior consultation (Fontana and Grugel 2016). The Inter-American Court of Human Rights has also been actively responding to conflicts highlighting the right of Indigenous and tribal communities to FPIC in the context of disputes over land (Hays and Kronik 2020). For instance, Guatemalan and Honduran organizations have filed cases against their respective governments to the IACHR alleging anomalies in relation to the organization of prior consultations. In Mexico, prior consultations are a comparatively underdeveloped policy instrument, though they are gaining more importance in the context of the AMLO and Sheinbaum administrations.

Several scholars have studied the ways in which prior consultations have been organized at the local level and the politics surrounding them. Drawing on ethnographic fieldwork surrounding the organization of prior consultations in Bolivia's mining sector, Perreault (2015) argues that "public consultation circumscribes and depoliticizes unequal and unjust social relations, in an attempt to legitimize extractive activities" (Perreault 2015, 434). They have become, he argues, "a technology of government par excellence" that has "yet to live up to its liberatory promise" (Perreault 2015, 449). Larsen and Gilbert (2020) suggest that C169 has become essential "in mediating the encounter between private sector investors and Indigenous communities" (p. 86). In a similar spirit, Dunlap (2018) argues that in the context of widespread opposition to the construction of wind energy turbines in the Isthmus of Tehuantepec in Mexico, the FPIC procedure was wielded "as a counter-insurrectionary device to pacify opposition and legitimize controversial development projects" (Dunlap 2018, 90). In some cases, then, prior consultations can facilitate a sort of "dispossession with consultation," and in the process, become technologies of governance that attempt to legitimize the expansion of extractive projects by highlighting the participatory mechanisms they were subjected to.

FPIC is often framed as an inherently virtuous tool that will indisputably serve the collective good, and that Indigenous people will not try to pursue their individual interests. As Fontana and Grugel (2016) suggest, "it is almost certainly scholarly 'otherization' of indigeneity that leads to expectations of harmony from the process, not 'normal' political conflict" (p. 257). Their research in Bolivia shows that in the context of the infamous TIPNIS conflict in Bolivia, the politics surrounding prior consultation ended up exacerbating tensions rather than ameliorating them (Fontana and Grugel 2016, 253). In addition to channeling social discontent around extractive projects, "FPIC really rests on an assumption of clearly identified and static cultural identities . . . . when most ethnic identities are in fact fluid social constructions, dependent on politics and subject to change" (Fontana and Grugel 2016, 257). In short, researchers have demonstrated that prior consultations and FPIC are not neutral or unproblematic instruments.

The fact that in some countries conflicts over land and extractivism have disproportionately affected people who self-identify as Indigenous or tribal has contributed to the idea that Indigenous communities are uniquely concerned about environmental issues. There is often a romanticization and essentialization of Indigeneity that is reproduced by international institutions, including many documents published by the ILO and the World Bank. Indigenous communities in rural areas are imagined as ecologically minded and hence indispensable participants in struggles against climate change and environmental degradation (Shah 2007). Li's (2010) work reminds us of the importance of avoiding the conflation of Indigenous communities with harmonious groups that naturally prefer collective property, are innately ecological, and are homogeneous victims of external capitalist forces. Rather, she insists on paying attention to the microlevel dynamics of class differentiation that have shaped the experience of Indigenous and rural communities for centuries. These need to be understood alongside broader processes that affect them, including powerful domestic and transnational capital. Claiming ancestral ties to and rights over territories can be crucial for the political power and for the strategic framing of struggles of Indigenous and tribal peoples, but it can also be simplistic and inaccurate at the local level. Still, in granting privileged rights over "ancestral" land to self-identified Indigenous and tribal peoples, ILO Convention 169 firmly ties together the politics of identity construction, citizenship regimes, land tenure politics, and the political economy of extractivism. The next two sections detail how these ideas have played out in the Mexican context.

4 Mexico's Formal Engagement with ILO Convention No. 169

Predictably, there are myriad differences between the content of ILO Convention No. 169 in theory and how it has been applied at the local level upon ratification. As Larsen (2020) indicates, ratification is only the first step in a long process that raises manifold dilemmas and practical obstacles regarding the domestic implementation of international law. The ILO's work is done primarily via global standard setting and technical assistance, but it has no ability to "force" implementation of its conventions. The ILO does, however, supervise how its conventions are applied and has mechanisms to receive complaints when something is not being properly implemented. In the face of complaints, it is constrained to making requests and offering recommendations to the relevant states, but the way governments respond ultimately depends on their political will and priorities.

This second half of the Element addresses how the ideas of C169 have played out in Mexico, with special attention to the content of the complaints (i.e., "representations" in ILO parlance) filed by Mexican organizations regarding the aspects in which effective adoption has fallen short from their point of view. Section 4 summarizes Mexico's formal engagement with the ILO in relation to C169 as reflected in official representations. In Section 5, the content of these representations is the starting point for a more detailed analysis of the intersection of Indigenous identity politics and land disputes in Mexico, drawing on the three-pronged analytical framework laid out earlier. In dissecting the content of the limits of ILO Convention No. 169 in practice, I pay particular attention to the politics and history of Mexico's citizenship regime, its land tenure regime, and how this relates to the politics surrounding the construction of Indigenous identities and land claims.

Representations Filed by Mexican Organizations to the ILO

Article 22 of the ILO Constitution states that all member states have the obligation to submit reports to the ILO detailing the actions they have taken to implement all ratified Conventions. Thus, governments are expected to regularly send updates to the ILO delineating any progress or challenges faced with regard to the application of a particular Convention, both as part of domestic legal frameworks and public policies. The reports are then read by twenty independent legal experts who are part of the ILO's Committee of Experts on the Application of Conventions and Recommendations (CEACR). After reading the reports, the CEACR sometimes shares either "observations" or "direct requests" to the relevant country. These comments are non-binding and are simply meant to be constructive suggestions for domestic authorities to consider. A selected number of reports are also examined by a tripartite standing committee called the Conference Committee on the Application of Standards (CAS). Any employer or worker association can submit so-called "representations" (i.e., complaints) to the ILO whenever they believe that a member state has failed to effectively observe a ratified Convention. Once these are approved by the ILO's Governing Body, the ILO at times shares the content of the complaints with the relevant state, including any accompanying observation or direct request. Through an analysis of the documents published by the ILO's supervisory system, in this section, I address the ways in which the ideas of ILO Convention No. 169 have influenced claims over land based on Indigeneity in Mexico, as well as their limitations in practice.

Globally, there has been an unusually high number of representations filed by both national and international trade unions in relation to the perceived inappropriate application of ILO Convention 169 (Larsen and Gilbert 2020). "Almost all the representations alleged, and proved, failure by the governments concerned to involve the indigenous peoples correctly in consultations as required by Article 6 of the Convention, either on land rights and resource exploitation, or on constitutional, legislative, and administrative amendments that directly affected their interests" (Swepston 2020, 118). Mexico has filed the highest number of complaints to the ILO in the entire world (a total of seven representations).[5] Thus, Mexico is the country that has most systematically engaged with the ILO supervisory system in relation to C169. Having examined all the representations filed by Mexican organizations to the ILO as of 2023, as well as the observations and direct requests made to the Mexican government, next, I summarize some of the recurring issues that emerge in these documents in relation to land conflicts, extractive industries, and the lack of systematic prior consultations.

As mentioned earlier, territorial disputes at the intersection of Indigeneity and the political economy of extractivism are institutionally intertwined with labor politics due to the structure and history of the ILO. Even though Indigenous organizations do not have formal and official channels of communication with the ILO, they sometimes append communications to documents filed by labor organizations. In this way, what is (in)visible and/or important to the ILO depends on the existence of alliances and direct communication channels between Indigenous organizations and labor organizations at the national level. Unsurprisingly, then, there are dozens of examples of land disputes and anti-extractive struggles in which Indigenous and tribal peoples participate that are not part of the conversation within the ILO because they lack relationships or communication channels with relevant labor unions that do have a voice at the ILO. Still, numerous labor organizations have served as intermediaries for communicating some of Mexico's Indigenous people's demands to the ILO, including unions composed of education workers, metal workers, newspaper workers, electricians, telephone workers, and municipal service workers.[6]

---

[5] In comparison, Argentina has filed two representations, Bolivia one, Brazil two, Chile two, Colombia two, Denmark one, Ecuador two, Guatemala one, Nepal one, and Peru three.

[6] The labor organizations that have filed representations in relation to the inappropriate application of ILO Convention 169 in Mexico include: (1) FAT, Authentic Labor Front (*Frente Auténtico del Trabajo*); (2) SNTE, National Trade Union of Education Workers (*Sindicato Nacional de Trabajadores de la Educación*); (3) SAINAH, Academic Trade Union of the National Institute of Anthropology and History (*Sindicato de Académicos del Instituto Nacional de Antropología e Historia*); (4) STUNAM, Union of Workers in the National Autonomous University of Mexico (*Sindicato de Trabajadores de la Universidad Nacional Autónoma de México*); (5) STIMAHCS, Radical Trade Union of Metal and Associated Workers (*Sindicato de Trabajadores de la Industria Metálica, Acero, Hierro, Conexos y Similares)*; (6) SITRAJOR, Independent Union of Workers of La Jornada (*Sindicato Independiente de Trabajadores de La Jornada*); (7) SME, Mexican Electricians' Union (*Sindicato Mexicano de Electricistas*); (8) STRM, Telephone Workers' Union (*Sindicato de Telefonistas de la República Mexicana*); (9) SINTCB, Independent National Trade Union of the Colegio de Bachilleres (*Sindicato Independiente Nacional de Trabajadores del Colegio de Bachilleres*); and (10) STSEMT, State and Municipal Services Workers' Union of Tabasco (Sindicato de Trabajadores al Servicio del Estado y los Municipios de Tabasco).

Summary of Core Points Made in the Representations Filed by Mexican Organizations

The territorial disputes that are mentioned in the seven representations filed to the ILO by the Mexican organization are summarized throughout this subsection (note that the third one listed includes four representations in the same ILO report). I first highlight the major points made in all representations in chronological order. I then discuss crosscutting themes that emerge across various representations.

1. *Representation filed by the National Trade Union of Education Workers (SNTE) in support of the Union of Huichol Indigenous Communities of Jalisco claiming rights to ancestral territories.*

The ILO received this representation in 1997 and published a report about it in 1998. The Huichol communities of Jalisco make two core points in this document. First, they make historical claims to territory, particularly over the town of San Andrés de Cohamiata. Secondly, they insist that there had been a lack of prior consultations and FPIC in relation to land conflicts. They petitioned the government to return 22,000 hectares of land to San Andrés, which the federal government allegedly adjudicated to mixed (*mestizo*) communities in the 1960s. The evidence they provided to the Agrarian Tribunal included titles to the land granted by the Spanish Crown in 1725, a land survey from 1809, and federal government documents from 1960 that admitted that San Andrés Cohamiata held title to 129,000 hectares of land. They argue they have the right to possess the ancestral lands they have historically inhabited. The Mexican authorities have systematically failed to respond to their demands.

2. *Representation filed by the Radical Trade Union of Metal and Associated Workers (STIMAHCS) in support of Chinantecs in Oaxaca demanding land after having been displaced by a dam built by the Mexican government.*

The ILO received the representation in 1998 and published a report in 1999. It describes the forced relocation of 5,000 Chinantec Indigenous families due to the construction of the Cerro del Oro dam in San Lucas Ojitlán, Oaxaca. The federal government ordered the construction of the dam in 1972 in the Papaloapan River, which flooded the region of San Lucas Ojitlán. At the time, the government promised compensation for loss of homes, lands, and crops. A presidential decree promised 260,000 hectares of land in Uxpanapa Valley, Veracruz, as compensation; however, they were only given 90,000 hectares. They were also promised infrastructure projects, including a paved main road, basic public services, and development projects to improve their living and health conditions, but these promises were unfulfilled. Through this representation, Chinantec communities requested the entirety of the lands promised to them. They too highlighted the lack of prior consultations and FPIC in the face of relocation.

3. *Representation filed by the Union of Academics of the National Institute of Anthropology and History (SAINAH), the Union of Workers of the Autonomous University of Mexico (STUNAM), the Independent Union of Workers of La Jornada (SITRAJOR), and the Authentic Workers' Front (FAT)[7], all alleging non-observance by Mexico of ILO Convention 169.*

The four unions submitted separate communications in 2001, and the ILO published a report addressing three of them in 2004. These representations foreground the systematic violation of Article 6 of the ILO Convention in relation to the right to prior consultation throughout the legislative process leading to the 2001 Constitutional Reform on Indigenous Rights. They argue that there were flagrant incompatibilities between the 2001 Constitutional reforms and ILO Convention 169, as will be addressed in more detail later in the Element. They also highlight the militarization of Indigenous communities, especially in the states of Oaxaca, Guerrero, and Chiapas, as well as the frequent land thefts and conflicts that exist in Indigenous territories.

4. *Representation filed by the Union of Metal, Steel, Iron and Allied Workers (STIMAHCS), alleging failure to observe certain provisions of ILO Convention 169, especially in relation to the construction of the Isthmus of Tehuantepec highway in Oaxaca.*

The ILO received the representation in 2002 and published a report in 2006. It makes three core points: First, it highlights the systematic violation of the right to prior consultation in the construction of the Isthmus of Tehuantepec highway. Second, it discusses the fact that the right of Indigenous peoples to decide their own development priorities is repeatedly infringed upon in Mexico. Third, it describes the intensification of pre-existing agrarian conflicts and the creation of new conflicts surrounding claims to ancestral lands.

In addition to the representations summarized above, the CEACR also published a total of fourteen observations and eleven direct requests to the Mexican government as of 2023. Other land conflicts that are mentioned as part of CEACR observations and direct requests in some detail include: land disputes in Chihuahua involving Tarahumara communities and extractive

---

[7] The Mexican government claimed that the FAT could not make representations, arguing that it is not a true industrial association of workers as delineated under Article 24 of the ILO Constitution. The ILO agreed with the Mexican government's point and discarded the representation drafted by the FAT in 2001.

industries; territorial disputes involving Huichol Indigenous people from Jalisco; and multiple conflicts surrounding the Tehuantepec Isthmus megaproject in the states of Oaxaca and Veracruz. Here I detail some of the recurring themes that appear in all these documents, as they help us better understand the reach and challenges regarding the implementation of ILO Convention 169 in a specific context. Generally, two of the themes that emerge most frequently in the representations and the CEACR's observations and direct requests are: (1) disputes over the legal definition of Indigeneity and its implications; and (2) the lack of properly organized prior consultations surrounding territorial conflicts, some of which involve criminal actors and drug cartels. The objective hereafter is not to provide detailed analyses of each of the cases mentioned, but rather, to address the key themes that they raise with regard to the challenges of implementing the ideas of ILO Convention 169 at the local level, considering the framework laid out earlier.

One of the issues that is addressed repeatedly in ILO requests since the 1990s is the question of rights to natural resources found in Indigenous lands. In 1993, for example, the CEACR stated:

> The Committee has found no indication from the information provided in the report that special measures have been taken to safeguard the rights of indigenous peoples to the natural resources pertaining to their lands. The Government has provided no information on any measures which would ensure shared responsibility for management and conservation of resources, or that the indigenous communities would benefit from the exploitation of resources on their lands, and the Government has made no mention in its report of any programme except expropriation and compensation as a response to the possibility of exploitation of the natural resources pertaining to the lands of indigenous communities (1993 CEACR Direct Request).

For example, one of the specific conflicts that illustrates this point is the case of disputes between Tarahumara communities in that the state of Chihuahua in Northern Mexico with mining and logging multinational companies. In a representation, the FAT alleged that these industries had "caused deforestation which in turn has led to an increase in drought conditions and placed the survival of the Rarámuri people in jeopardy" (1998 CEACR observation). The FAT further argued that:

> In 1995 the International Paper Company obtained contracts in the Tarahumara range, through local landowners, the authorities responsible for communal land and a forestry official, for the purchase of 75 per cent of the timber and cellulose from communal lands, since Mexican legislation does not establish restrictions on direct contracts between private enterprises and authorities responsible for common lands (1998 CEACR Direct Request).

In response to the representation filed by the FAT, the CEACR made the following observation to the Mexican government:

> The Committee requests the Government to make full use of appropriate procedures for consulting the indigenous communities who may be affected by any development projects on their lands or by the award of any concessions for the exploitation of natural resources on lands belonging to or traditionally occupied by those peoples (1998 CEACR observation).

Despite numerous observations and requests made by the ILO, the conflict worsened and became increasingly violent, to the point that it was brought to the Inter-American Court of Human Rights. Land disputes, particularly in relation to logging permits, intensified and became intertwined with territorial disputes between drug cartels, especially those involved in the traffic of opium poppy and marihuana to the USA (CIDH 2016). The CEACR noted that "In March 2017 the Inter-American Court of Human Rights adopted provisional measures in favour of the members of the Choréachi indigenous community of the Sierra Tarahumara in the State of Chihuahua in view of the situation of violence caused by attempts by criminal organizations to occupy the community's lands" (2019 CEACR observation).

The ongoing territorial disputes between drug cartels and the Mexican government are another critical barrier for the effective implementation of the ideas of C169. As disputes between cartels and the state intensified, so did the interest from cartels in controlling rural areas, especially the mountainous regions in both the north and the south, many of which are home to Indigenous communities. The challenges to internal sovereignty posed by drug cartels across vast swaths of Mexico's territory evidently show that the state lacks the capacity to guarantee respect of territorial rights in the first place, Indigenous or non-Indigenous.

Various scholars have researched the implications of the drug wars on Indigenous communities. Navarro-López (2024), for instance, traces the forced internal displacement processes that have affected many of Chiapas' Indigenous communities. In certain areas, cartels have also become interested in profiting from extractive industries, notably mining. Santaolalla (2023) discusses how, in the southwestern state of Guerrero, mining companies thrive despite the brutal violence linked to drug cartels. In fact, cartels often extort and demand so-called "payment of dues" from mining companies. In some cases, cartels have done the dirty work of displacing inhabitants from a certain area of land where there is interest in establishing a new extractive project. Like in Chiapas, both the mining industry and the territorial disputes between drug cartels have led to high levels of forced displacements. Ley et al. (2019) investigated "why some indigenous communities in Mexico have been able to resist drug cartels' attempts to take over their local governments, populations, and territories while others have not" (p. 181). They find that "the communities most able to resist narco conquest are those that have a history of social mobilization, expanding village-level indigenous customary traditions into regional ethnic autonomy regimes" (p. 181).

Another territorial conflict discussed in significant detail by the CEACR involves the Union of Huichol Indigenous Communities of Jalisco. This case was initially brought to the ILO's attention through a representation filed in 1998 by the education workers' union, SNTE. It involves claims to land that huicholes "traditionally" occupied, but that they lost to other non-Indigenous people in the area. The Huichol communities demanded "the return to the Huichol community of San Andrés de Cohamiata of 22,000 hectares adjudicated by the federal Government to agrarian groups in the 1960s" (2005 CEACR observation). The Huicholes argue that existing titling removed "43 per cent of its ancestral lands recognized in titles dating back to the colonial era" (2005 CEACR observation). Furthermore, they claimed that a forestry concession had been unlawfully granted in land they consider traditional. In 2005, the CEACR urged the Mexican government to consider "assigning additional lands to the Huichol people when they do not have the area necessary for providing the essentials of normal existence, or for any possible increase in their numbers, as provided in Article 19 of the Convention" (2005 CEACR observation).

In 2008, the Huichol case was again brought up in representations. It illustrates the thorny issue of determining "traditional occupation" in seeking rights to ownership and possession of land. The SNTE insisted that

> for the time being, the agrarian legislation does not provide for adequate procedures referred to under *Article 14(3)* of the Convention to recognize land traditionally occupied by indigenous peoples, and that for the judges, only the official documents are valid .... The SNTE adds that, although there was considerable evidence that the Huicholes had lived on the lands from time immemorial, as shown by the existence of titles granted by the Spanish Crown, as well as historical and anthropological studies, this was not enough because there were no procedures in national law to establish a link between the facts as presented and international standards (2008 CEACR observation).

The conflict has been unresolved for decades, despite both national and international attention to the case and repeated expressions of "concern" published by the ILO.

In addition to the complicated question of proving and defending land based on "traditional occupation," the other related challenge in the context of territorial disputes revolves around the organization of prior consultations. The CEACR frequently highlighted the lack of established procedures for organizing prior consultations with Indigenous communities as a key weakness. Most of the representations filed with the ILO by Mexican organizations stress the lack of prior consultations. Due to the lack of well-specified rules and procedures for who and how these should be carried out, it is common for the state to establish who has the right to participate in a way that strongly affects the outcome. Thus, in 2007, the CEACR reiterated:

> Noting that a large proportion of the representations and communications addressed by the Committee refer to consultation and participation, the Committee requests the Government to provide information on the specific measures adopted to set up appropriate bodies and machinery for consultation and participation, to seek solutions that are inclusive of the various interests at stake on the basis of dialogue, to prevent the recurrence of disputes relating to the issue of consultation and participation and to keep the Committee informed in this respect (2007 CEACR observation).

The lack of prior consultations is repeatedly brought up in relation to conflicts involving the Tehuantepec Isthmus mega-project, for example. This is an ambitious infrastructure project that has gone through various phases and continues to be polemic to this day. It includes highways and railways connecting Mexico's Atlantic and Pacific coasts through the states of Oaxaca and Veracruz, in addition to industrial parks and energy projects. In the late 1990s, the FAT highlighted that these projects were being introduced "without any consultations with the indigenous peoples in the region on the social, spiritual, cultural and environmental impact of this project on the land and the people's way of life" (1998 CEACR observation). By 2011, the Mexican government claimed that it was working on more systematically organizing prior consultations. The 2013–14 energy reform incorporated requirements for prior consultations more explicitly, particularly for hydrocarbon or electricity industry projects.

Even though prior consultations were acknowledged as an important element of a new type of relationship between the Mexican state and Indigenous populations, it wasn't a prioritized policy instrument. It wasn't until the 2013–14 energy reform that secondary legislation was passed about the need to carry out prior consultations before embarking on new energy projects. Article 120, almost at the very end of the Law, notes that whenever hydrocarbon industry projects affect Indigenous peoples and communities, the Energy Secretariat must organize a free, prior, and informed consent consultation, as is stipulated by ILO Convention 169 (Ley de Hidrocarburos 2014). The goal of the consultation is ostensibly to reach agreements and consent. Between 2014 and 2017, the Energy Secretariat reported that they had carried out fourteen consultations related to energy projects (Sener 2018). Still, there is nothing in the Law that provides details about how to proceed in cases in which communities might be against the expansion of hydrocarbon activities on their land. As of 2025, the ruling party Morena is attempting to more systematically regulate and carry out prior consultations with indigenous communities, but it's too soon to make conclusions about their potential role.

5 ILO Convention No. 169 in Practice in Mexico

Mexico ratified ILO Convention 169 over thirty years ago, and yet this has not palpably contributed to the defense or restoration of "ancestral" lands claimed by Indigenous peoples. High-ranking politicians are aware of the Convention but have not prioritized its application. Rather, they have intentionally attempted to circumvent its more radical ideas. In an interview with high-ranking politician Lourdes Melgar (the Electricity Undersecretary during the Peña Nieto administration), she recognized that even though the ideas of ILO Convention 169 are supposed to be the law in Mexico, "nobody pays attention to them."[8] What happened with the commitment the government made with the EZLN in 1996 to respect C169, and what does that tell us about the promise and limits of enforcing the Convention? To best answer this question, I first provide a brief historical overview of the intersection of Indigeneity and agrarian struggles in Mexico. Following the framework laid out in the introduction, I then highlight the major obstacles and limits of C169 in practice by highlighting the interaction between: (1) the specific ways in which Indigenous and tribal identities have been constructed in Mexico over time; (2) the particularities of Mexico's version of a multicultural citizenship regime; and (3) Mexico's regnant land tenure regimes. As will be further explained below, I suggest that the legal prioritization of extractive industries in Mexico's prevailing land tenure regime, in conjunction with a relatively weak multicultural citizenship regime that is not accompanied by land tenure options that recognize Indigeneity as the basis upon which to obtain land, have been critical obstacles for the ability of self-identified Indigenous groups to successfully secure rights over ancestral lands.

Indigeneity and Mexico's Agrarian Struggles in Historical Perspective

Details about Mexican agrarian history are beyond the scope of this Element, but for contextualization purposes, here I summarize some of the key features of

---

[8] Interview with Lourdes Melgar Palacios, 2019.

Mexico's land tenure regimes from the colonial era to the twenty-first century. This is significant for understanding the historical roots of the inexistence of a land tenure option specifically designed for Indigenous and tribal peoples in Mexico at the national level. I pay particular attention to the key reforms introduced in the context of neoliberalization, especially those that directly affected Indigenous people and contemporary territorial disputes. I also highlight the connection made by Mexican Indigenous organizations in recent decades between Indigenous peoples' rights and territorial rights.

Colonial Mexico was founded on a dual political system, each with its own set of rules and assumptions. On the one hand, there was the "Republic of Spaniards" (*República de españoles*) and on the other, the "Republic of Indians" (*República de indios*). Thus, colonial Mexico was built upon an institutionalized distinction between natives and colonizers. This dual system set the foundation for Mexico's colonial and post-colonial land tenure regimes. As part of this model, the Spanish crown resettled and concentrated Indigenous people in what they called "Indian villages" (*pueblos de indios*) during the early colonial period, to allegedly more efficiently govern, control, exploit, and evangelize the Indigenous populations. This forced relocation of people was essential for the design and reproduction of the labor regime through which colonial plunder and dispossession occurred. As Loveman (2014) notes, "Official racial classification in colonial Latin America was integral to a system of imperial rule designed, in the first instance, to facilitate orderly extraction of agricultural, mineral, and fiscal resources from the colonial domains" (pp. 43–44).

The dual system of Indigenous communal tenure alongside Spanish and criollo landholdings introduced during colonialism continues to have implications for contemporary land ownership patterns and agrarian struggles. "During the three centuries of colonial rule, the Spanish Crown distributed thousands of titles and *escrituras* (deeds) that laid the legal groundwork for the present-day agrarian communities" (Assies 2008, 35). Many ongoing land disputes make reference to colonial-era land titles as evidence of "ancestral" ownership. In reality, these titles are colonial constructs that may or may not overlap precisely with pre-colonial habitation patterns or property ideas, but they have nonetheless become the closest thing to legal "proof" used by Indigenous and tribal peoples trying to demonstrate that they are/were the "original" residents of particular territories.

In the post-colonial era, the dramatic land concentration and dispossession of Indigenous territories that benefited the criollo and Spanish elite persisted and intensified. In the nineteenth century, liberal legislation favoring the privatization of land and the creation of individual property holders further contributed to the erosion of what remained of communal and Indian forms of land tenure. The deepening of land concentration in the hands of a few set the stage for the Mexican Revolution and led to widespread demands for agrarian reform. Famously, revolutionaries led by Emiliano Zapata in the early twentieth century placed demands for land at the center of their political agenda, under the banner "Land and liberty."

In the aftermath of the Mexican Revolution, calls for agrarian reform were high on the political agenda, including demands for state recognition of collectively held land. An ambitious agrarian reform program was introduced by the Lázaro Cárdenas administration in the late 1930s, including state-sanctioned forms of communal ownership. Indian villages under colonial rule usually contained an *ejido*, a term originally used to refer to communal land assigned for livestock. This term was refashioned in the post-Revolutionary period to denote collective land holdings more generally. After the Revolution, *ejidos* (collective land holdings) and communal lands were officially recognized and institutionalized by the state, supported by Article 27 of the 1917 Constitution. The two communal forms of land tenure established during the post-Revolutionary period, *ejidos* and agrarian communities (*comunidades agrarias*), were not linked explicitly to Indigenous identity, but rather to peasantness. In practice, however, these collective land tenure institutions oftentimes did overlap with Indigenous communities. As a result, the *ejidos* and agrarian communities indirectly protected Indigenous land from privatization to some degree and served as a place where Indigenous culture and practices could reproduce themselves. Still, the justification for the agrarian reform at the time was not primarily about the defense of Indigenous people's rights, at least discursively. It was about social justice, inequality, anti-imperialism, liberty, and the perception that land should be owned by "those that work it." Nonetheless, by the 1990s, the most widespread form of land tenure for Indigenous peoples was *ejidos*, followed by private property and then by communal property.

As previously noted, the strengthening of ethnic based claims in the late twentieth century across Latin America coincided with the deepening of neoliberal reforms. In 1991, there was a reform to section VII of article 27 of the Mexican Constitution that was of utmost significance for territorial claims linked to Indigeneity, and for the possibility of privatizing land previously held collectively. The reform removed the "imprescriptibility, unattachability, and inalienability" Constitutional clause in relation to *ejidos*, the vital phrase that safeguarded communal land from privatization for decades. Paradoxically, the ratification of ILO Convention 169 in Mexico happened the same year that the state began to allow for unprecedented opportunities to privatize collectively held land.

The 1994 Zapatista uprising placed Indigenous peoples' rights and demands center stage in the national political agenda. The movement famously went public the same day that NAFTA went into effect. The triumphant "end of history" spirit that some advocates of neoliberalization espoused after the collapse of the Soviet Union was quickly shattered in Mexico in the face of the EZLN rebellion and the concurrent financial crisis of 1994. After a long and delicate negotiation process, the San Andrés Peace Accords were signed between the EZLN and the Mexican government on February 16, 1996. The hope was that these agreements would prevent the reignition of an armed conflict. The content of ILO Convention No. 169 played an important role as a document of reference during the negotiations of the Peace Accords. In fact, the Convention is directly mentioned in the Accords, especially in relation to territorial rights and self-determination issues. The agreement was that the Accords would translate into legislative reforms in upcoming years, which would establish the foundation of a new type of relationship between the state and Indigenous peoples, both at the national and state levels. The government made two key commitments to the EZLN: First, it would introduce legislation to recognize Indigenous peoples in the Mexican Constitution (until then, not even mentioned in the text); and second, it would guarantee that prior consultations would be organized whenever any policies, laws, or programs were to affect Indigenous peoples (San Andrés Accords 1996). Relatedly, the State would acknowledge Indigenous peoples' right to self-determination.

For the ELZN, disputes over the regnant land tenure regime, including the aforementioned reform to Article 27 of the Mexican Constitution, were and are intimately tied to the struggle for Indigenous peoples' territorial rights and to the broader need to address systemic inequalities. The very first point of the San Andres Accords stated: "The EZLN delegation insists on pointing out the lack of attention given to the severe national agrarian problem, and to the need to reform Article 27 of the Constitution, which should once again capture the spirit of Emiliano Zapata, summarized in two basic demands: the land is for that who works it, and Land and Liberty" (San Andrés Accords 1996). Unlike the early twentieth-century followers of Emiliano Zapata, however, the EZLN placed Indigeneity at the center of its discourse and demands. The EZLN's public appearance followed years of Indigenous peoples' rights activism across the country. In 1992, for example, there was a reform to Article 4 of the Mexican Constitution that acknowledged Mexico's multicultural composition, but it fell short in terms of explicitly delineating Indigenous peoples' rights.

The COCOPA, or Commission for Peace and Reconciliation, was entrusted with proposing constitutional reforms drawing on C169 and the San Andrés Accords, an initiative that the EZLN initially supported. After many polarized debates, a watered-down version eventually became the 2001 reform, which was publicly rejected by the EZLN, the CNI (Mexico's National Congress of Indigenous People), and the Millennium Conference of Indigenous Peoples. As the summaries of the representations provided earlier make clear, the 2001 reform was, and continues to be, considered antithetical to the ideas of ILO Convention No. 169. The 2001 reform was denounced by the EZLN and multiple Indigenous organizations as being inconsistent with the spirit of both the Peace Accords and of ILO Convention No. 169. Despite initial optimism regarding the recognition of Indigenous people's rights in the late 1990s, there has been little progress in relation to the implementation of C169 in Mexico. To understand why, the following subsections address the limits of the Convention in practice, considering the politics of Mexico's state-sponsored definition of Indigeneity, the features of its version of a multicultural citizenship regime, and the constraints related to the regnant land tenure regime.

The Politics of State-Sponsored Definitions of Indigeneity in Mexico

In multicultural citizenship regimes, wherein special rights are granted based on Indigenous or tribal identity, the official definition of Indigeneity has critical political and material implications. As discussed in the introductory section, ILO Convention 169 states that self-identification as Indigenous or tribal should be the criterion through which to determine whether the Convention is relevant to particular people or not. Self-identification has not historically been the metric, however, whereby the modern Mexican state has defined Indigeneity. Institutionalizing the ILO's definition has been a slow, polemic, and difficult process. Additionally, even as the Mexican government begins to utilize the self-identification metric, this does not guarantee that it is accompanied by the recognition of the manifold rights delineated in C169 for the relevant people.

Shortly after Mexico ratified C169, the ILO began pressuring the Mexican government to incorporate the "self-identification" criteria for categorizing people as Indigenous or tribal. This theme was a recurring one throughout the numerous requests made by the CEACR to Mexico since the 1990s. The CEACR's first "direct request" from 1993, for instance, begins by celebrating the fact that in 1991 there was a reform to article four of the Mexican Constitution that states that Mexico "has a multicultural composition based originally on its indigenous peoples." At the same time, it expressed concern over the fact that in Mexico, the use of an Indigenous language continued to be the primary criterion by which the government classified people as Indigenous at the time, which undermined the criteria of self-identification delineated in the Convention.

In the aftermath of the 2001 reform to Article 2 of the Mexican Constitution on Indigenous issues, the CEACR continued to critique the Mexican state's definition of Indigeneity, particularly its assumptions regarding the relationship between Indigeneity, linguistic criteria, and settlement in a particular territory. The CEACR stated:

> *Definition and self-identification.* The Committee notes with interest that article 2 of the reform provides that awareness of indigenous identity shall be a fundamental criterion in determining those persons to whom the provisions on indigenous peoples apply. Article 2 then defines the component communities of an indigenous people as "those which form a social, economic and cultural whole ... settled in a territory". The Committee also notes the fifth paragraph of article 2 ... shall take into account, in addition to the general principles set out in the previous paragraphs of this article, ethno-linguistic criteria and physical location." The Committee would be grateful if the Government would provide information in its next report on the manner in which ethno-linguistic requirements and physical location are interpreted, and in particular on how recognition is ensured of the membership of those indigenous peoples or communities which have lost their ancestral land and have resettled in urban areas (2001 CEACR Direct Request).

In short, for the ILO, it was problematic that the Mexican state continued to rely on ethno-linguistic criteria and physical location to determine who is Indigenous or not. This way of understanding Indigeneity was roughly a century old. Ever since formal censuses in Mexico began classifying people as Indigenous in 1895, language had been the main criterion for the state-sanctioned definition of Indigeneity. As Loveman (2014) describes, "The 1895 Mexican census report presented tables titled 'population according to habitually-spoken language [*idioma habitual*],' with numbers of speakers of various indigenous languages broken down by state and municipality. The list was extensive, including twenty different indigenous languages" (p. 135).

By the early twenty-first century, despite pressure from the ILO and various local Indigenous people's rights movements, the Mexican state continued to use ethnolinguistic criteria alongside physical settlement as the way to classify people as Indigenous. As Li (2010) notes, "in many contexts, the only properly indigenous person is a person embedded in a group and a place" (p. 399). This link is reproduced in the discourse and logic of much of the international human rights framework and is also implicit in

Mexico's Constitution. The rights outlined in the UN Declaration on the Rights of Indigenous Peoples, for example, apply to groups, not to individuals. "If a group is fractured, or favours individualized property, or an individual acts alone, indigenous rights that are contingent on the existence of a collectivity evaporate" (Li 2010, 399). What happens then with people that self-identify as Indigenous but live in urban areas and have weak or no ties to ancestral territories?[9]

The National Institute of Statistics and Geography (INEGI), the institution that organizes Mexico's national censuses, ultimately incorporated the criteria of self-designation as Indigenous for a sample of the population during the 2010 census. In a 2011 Direct Request, the CEACR observed:

> In the specific case of the XIIth General Census of the Population and Family, undertaken in 2010, two questionnaires were used: a basic questionnaire intended for the whole of the population, in which the linguistic criterion was used, and an extended questionnaire intended for a sample of the population, in which the criterion of self-designation was applied. The population sample represented approximately 10 per cent of the total population of the country and was representative in national, state, and municipal terms. The Committee notes that, according to the information gathered in the XIIth Census, 15.7 million people aged 3 and above identified themselves as indigenous. Of these, 6.6 million speak an indigenous language. According to the Census, the federated entities with the highest percentage of indigenous people are Yucatán (62 per cent) and Oaxaca (58 per cent). The Committee recalls that *Article 1(2)* of the Convention provides that self-identification as indigenous or tribal shall be regarded as a fundamental criterion for determining the groups to which the provisions of the Convention apply. *Under these conditions, the Committee invites the Government to include the question on self-designation in the basic questionnaire intended for the whole of the population in future population censuses that are carried out in the country with a view to compiling the most accurate possible data on the number of persons who identify themselves as indigenous* (2011 CEACR Direct Request).

As is evident in these comments, the incorporation of the self-identification metric dramatically raised the number of Indigenous peoples in Mexico, and hence, the material and political repercussions in terms of rights and potential land claims could be momentous.

---

[9] According to the ILO, "Over 73.4 per cent of the global indigenous population live in rural areas, but there are substantial regional variations. The highest proportion of indigenous peoples residing in rural areas is found in Africa (82.1percent), followed by Asia and the Pacific (72.8 per cent) and Europe and Central Asia (66.4 per cent). Conversely, in Latin America and the Caribbean and in Northern America, a majority of indigenous peoples are urban dwellers (52.2 per cent and 69.0 per cent respectively). The data show that the higher the level of income, the lower the share of indigenous peoples residing in the countryside" (ILO 2019, 3).

In 2015, the Mexican government finally incorporated self-classification as Indigenous for the entire population as part of its 2015 Inter-census survey. In a 2019 request, the CEACR touched on this theme, affirming:

> The Committee notes in this regard that the Inter-census Survey 2015 included the criterion of self-classification as indigenous, based on which it was found that 25,694,928 people classified themselves as being indigenous, that is 21.5 per cent of the national population, while based on the criterion of indigenous households, the indigenous population was quantified as 12,025,947 persons, representing 10.1 per cent of the whole of the population in the country. *The Committee welcomes the use of the criterion of self-classification for the identification of the indigenous population in the country and requests the Government to provide examples of the manner in which this criterion is used to determine the beneficiaries of policies and programmes intended for indigenous and Afro-Mexican peoples* (2019 CEACR Direct Request).

In line with the ILO's preference, the 2020 census utilized the self-identification criteria for the entire population. As a result of this change, the total number of people classified as Indigenous doubled in comparison to twenty years earlier. In the year 2000, the Mexican state estimated that there were 12.7 million Indigenous people, roughly 10 percent of the total national population. By 2024, using the self-identification criteria, the number is now 25 million, around 20 percent of the population.

Alongside pressure to institutionalize self-identification as the metric whereby to categorize someone as Indigenous or not, there was also a burgeoning movement calling for the recognition, rights, and institutional visibility of Afro-Mexicans. Thus, as can be seen in the comment above from the 2019 CEACR direct request, the incorporation of Afro-Mexicans into public discourse and census politics was a novelty. "Mexico conducted a national census in 2010 that made Indigenous peoples visible but not Afrodescendants. In 2013, Mexico announced plans for another census in 2015 that would enumerate Afrodescendants" (Loveman 2014, 255). The political and material implications of this change are yet to be seen. What is clear is that if being categorized as Indigenous, Afrodescendant, or tribal grants you special rights, it helps us understand why the politics surrounding the criteria of self-identification have been so contentious in Mexico. In short, a crucial issue to analyze when thinking about the role and limits of international law in the context of land disputes involving Indigenous and tribal populations is the national politics surrounding identity construction, and whether the state incentivizes or attempts to thwart the political salience of certain identities. It is also a key point of contention surrounding the reach and limitations of contemporary multicultural citizenship regimes.

Mexico's Multicultural Citizenship Regime

It was not until the early 1990s that the Mexican government named Indigenous peoples in the Constitution, and in 2001, it passed a Constitutional reform that explicitly recognized Indigenous peoples' rights. This reform laid the groundwork for Mexico's twenty-first century version of a multicultural citizenship regime. In theory, the recognition of "special" rights for Indigenous and tribal populations is allegedly meant to acknowledge, remedy, and address the implications of centuries of oppression and dispossession, brought to the national and international spotlight by the EZLN. Most Indigenous organizations and their allies, however, publicly disagreed with the content of the 2001 reform.

The 2001 reform to Article 2 of the Mexican Constitution, referred to colloquially as the "Indigenous Law," triggered heated debates nationwide. The critiques of its content point to the delicate politics surrounding the design and institutionalization of multicultural citizenship regimes. Article 2 of the Mexican Constitution, as formulated in 2001, read:

> The Mexican nation is one and indivisible. It is a pluricultural nation originally sustained by its indigenous peoples, which are those who descend from populations that lived in the country's present territory as colonization began and that conserve, in whole or in part, their own social, economic, cultural and political institutions. Indigenous communities are those that form a social, economic and cultural unit, are established in a territory, and recognize their own authorities according to their customs. Indigenous peoples rights to self-determination will be exercised in a constitutional framework of autonomy that guarantees national unity. The recognition of indigenous peoples and communities will be incorporated into state Constitutions and laws, which should take into consideration the aforementioned points, in addition to ethnolinguistic criteria and physical settlement (Article 2 of the Mexican Constitution).

Even though the article recognized the right to self-determination, there are other articles in the Constitution that limited the capacity of Indigenous communities to put it into practice, as will be elaborated upon in the next section. This Article was reformed in late 2024 in a way that is more akin to the spirit of C169, but it is evidently too soon to assess the implications of this change.

In addition to widespread condemnation of the way that the 2001 version of Article 2 defined Indigeneity, another aspect of the Mexican Constitution that has been severely criticized is the fact that it transferred the responsibility for delineating and enforcing the rights of Indigenous peoples and communities to state governments. By delegating responsibilities to the different states, it transformed Indigenous peoples' rights into a subnational issue, instead of a federal one. As a result, there is no nationally delineated strategy for making sure that the various points of ILO Convention No. 169 are systematically enforced. A major related limitation of this decentralized multicultural citizenship regime in the context of land conflicts is that it is not accompanied by a land tenure regime that facilitates the recognition and protection of land based on Indigeneity. Thus, Mexico's version of a multicultural citizenship regime is relatively weak at the federal level, and particularly timid with regard to land rights.

The reiterated mention of national unity in Article 2 of the Constitution speaks to the Mexican government's fears over the threat of secession based on Indigeneity, a particularly delicate issue in the aftermath of the Zapatista uprising. This same concern was at the core of debates over the wording of ILO Convention 169 in the 1980s, particularly regarding the use of the term "peoples" as opposed to "populations" in its title. Many delegates to the ILO were hesitant about using the term "peoples" because of the possibility of claiming sovereignty rights under international law. The debate was resolved by incorporating the following caveat in the Convention: "The use of the term 'peoples' in this convention shall not be construed as having any implications as regards the rights which may attach to the term under international law" (Anaya 1996, 49). In Mexico, this tension is reflected in the choice of the word "populations" as opposed to "peoples" in the Constitutional reform. As Speed and Sierra (2005) remind us, "human rights and multi-culturalism are discourses of both state power and indigenous resistance" (p.5). The next subsection details some of the key characteristics of Mexico's contemporary land tenure regime, in relation to the nature of its multicultural citizenship regime.

Mexico's Regnant Land Tenure Regime

Analyzing land tenure alternatives and the various laws and regulations that together result in a particular land regime is crucial for understanding the reach and limits of ILO Convention 169 in the context of territorial struggles. Whereas a particular law or norm may claim that Indigenous peoples have self-determination and rights over their ancestral territories, there may be other laws that have primacy and hence override their supposed right to land. This is precisely what is happening in Mexico, where energy industries and mining have legal priority over all other land use according to the Constitution, so communities – Indigenous or otherwise – can be legally removed from their land if they happen to live in an area where a mining concession or an energy project has been authorized. In the Mexican context (and others), mining and hydrocarbon extraction have therefore sometimes been linked to dispossession of the rural poor in the name of development and economic growth.

The centrality of extractive industries to Mexico's political economy has radically shaped the features and politics of its land use priorities. Since the 1970s, energy industries and mining have enjoyed legal priority over any other imaginable land use. In 1977, amid the oil export bonanza, President López Portillo introduced a decree that reformed the secondary legislation of Constitutional Article 27 with regards to oil that states: "The petroleum industry is of public utility and has priority over any other subsoil and land use, including communal lands and *ejidos*. Thus, provisional occupation, definitive expropriation or legal compensation will follow whenever the Nation's oil industry requires it" (López Portillo 1977). In Mexico, classifying any activity as having "public utility" justifies the expropriation of land needed for its operations. This reform was fundamental for granting priority to oil extraction over all other potential land uses. The justification for the reform went as follows:

> In the face of the increasing internal and external demand, along with the important discoveries of hydrocarbons in our territory, the current moment demands an accelerated development of this industry in a short period of time. This implies inaugurating new oil fields, new processing plants, ancillary facilities, and pipelines. In order to successfully carry out such a program we need [...] legislation that establishes speedy mechanisms that allow Pemex to eliminate the serious problems that it could face, especially with regards to the necessary land occupations. The holistic development of the oil and petrochemical industries are of preferential interest and should rely on a legal framework that favors the rational and adequate exploitation of our oil wealth (López Portillo 1977).

In short, in Mexico, there are laws that override Indigenous people's alleged rights to ancestral territories, such as those stating that mining and hydrocarbon extraction are of the "national interest" and hence justify displacement or intervention in relevant areas.

Mexico's mining sector is currently at the center of dozens of territorial conflicts, many of which involve Indigenous communities. The mining sector is immense, with roughly 10 percent of the national territory currently under concession for mining purposes. Mining is almost entirely controlled by private companies, both domestic and transnational. Only hydrocarbon extraction and the transmission and distribution of electricity have priority over mining projects according to the law. If a mining project were to be incompatible with an energy project, then the energy project has priority. Mexico's 1992 Mining Law states that those with mining concessions have the right to expropriate or temporarily occupy the land of interest. They also have a right to use the water found in the area delineated for the mining project. Even though no new concessions have been granted since AMLO's election in 2018, no old ones have been revoked.

The rapid granting of mining concessions in the past three decades led to numerous socio-environmental and territorial conflicts. Over 400 community organizations against mining and extractive projects were created in Mexico between 2007 and 2017 (Lemus 2018). By 2017, there were at least 1,488 local conflicts related to mining, most of which were land dispossession complaints, but also included cases of grievances related to water struggles, pollution, the presence of armed groups, royalties, and deforestation (Lemus 2018). In 2018, a national coalition called REMA, the Mexican Network of People Affected by Mining (*Red Mexicana de Afectados por la Minería*), argued that there were 15,000 conflicts linked to mining in the country, in every state except one (Flores 2018). Between 2008 and 2018, at least 125 people were killed for defending territories and water in the face of extractive projects (Castellanos 2018). Of those killed, about 65 percent were Indigenous people, including nahuas, purepechas, raramuris, triquis, and wixarikas (Castellanos 2018). Displacement because of state-promoted infrastructure projects has also become increasingly sensitive in Indigenous communities.

Another critical limitation of Mexico's regnant land tenure regime is that there is no land tenure option specifically designed to protect and guarantee land titling for Indigenous communities. Mexico's version of a multicultural citizenship regime does not establish a differentiated right to land for Indigenous and tribal peoples. Indigenous peoples rely on a mix of other forms of collective land tenure and private ownership. As mentioned earlier, ILO Convention 169 went into effect while the paradigm-shifting 1991 reform to Mexico's agrarian legislation was passed. The reform to article 27 of the Constitution, allowing for the privatization of *ejido* land, initiated a long and arduous process of private land titling and parceling. It also provoked fierce debates regarding the future, virtues, and vices of communal landholding. The ILO's CEACR expressed concern for how the reform would affect Indigenous lands early on. In a 1993 direct request, they commented:

> The Committee notes that recent changes in the agrarian legislation would facilitate the alienation of the land of ejidos which was formerly inalienable, or its transformation to individual holdings which would also remove earlier restrictions on alienation. Please indicate the measures being taken in this connection to ensure that this does not lead to the loss of indigenous lands through persons not belonging to these peoples taking advantage of their

customs or lack of understanding to secure the ownership of these lands. The Committee notes in this connection that landlessness among indigenous peoples is closely linked to poverty and to migration toward the cities.... The Committee therefore requests the Government to indicate in its next report the extent to which the lands traditionally occupied by indigenous and tribal peoples has been identified and their rights protected (1993 CEACR direct request).

In practice, the protection of land "traditionally" occupied by Indigenous people was low on the government's agenda at the time. The 1994 Zapatista uprising helped change this to some degree, even though no concrete actions were taken to reverse this situation. The primacy of mining and energy industries in Mexico's political economy, compounded by the fact that there is no land tenure option specifically designed to safeguard Indigenous territories, is amongst the major obstacles for the capacity of Indigenous organizations to successfully obtain recognition of what they consider to be ancestral lands. The power and relative impunity of criminal organizations and drug cartels simultaneously complicate many Mexicans' ability to defend their land.

Almost thirty years have gone by since the signing of the San Andrés Peace accords in Mexico, but the supposed commitment by the Mexican government to align its domestic legal framework with the ideas of ILO Convention 169 has been slow and weak. In fact, Mexican organizations have filed the highest number of complaints to the ILO (a total of seven representations) in the world, alleging and proving failure of the Mexican government to correctly carry out consultations and to effectively address conflicts surrounding Indigenous land rights. The Mexican example makes it clear that we cannot understand the limits of ILO Convention No. 169 as a tool to make claims to ancestral territories without considering the constraints imposed by regnant land tenure regimes, and how that relates to the features of the regnant citizenship regime and the politics surrounding Indigenous identity. For the Mexican government, the prioritization of extractive industries has meant that the rights to land and self-determination of Indigenous populations have become secondary. In summary, the domestic implications of the ratification of ILO Convention No. 169 in Mexico have been limited in part because they have not been accompanied with the institutionalization of a land tenure regime that allows for the defense and recognition of land based on Indigeneity, and because there is an unwillingness from the state to challenge the power and prioritization of both private and public extractive industries and infrastructure projects in the reigning political economic model.

6 Conclusion: The Promise and Limits of ILO Convention 169 in Land Disputes

Like the broader international human rights regime, the reach and limitations of ILO Convention 169 are paradoxical and deeply shaped by local sociopolitical dynamics and power relations. This Element addressed the ways in which Indigenous peoples' rights as laid in ILO Convention 169 are mobilized at the local level in the context of territorial disputes, using the Mexican case as an example. It asked: How can we better understand the intersection of Indigenous identity politics, the international human rights regime, and land conflicts today, in Mexico and beyond? To best address this question, it proposed a three-pronged framework for the analysis of the intersection of territorial struggles and Indigenous identity politics, in both Mexico and elsewhere. The framework focuses on investigating the specificities and interconnections between: (1) citizenship regimes, (2) land tenure regimes, and (3) the politics surrounding the local construction of Indigeneity and tribal identities.

More precisely, I suggest tracing the interrelationships between these variables when trying to understand the reach and limits of the ideas espoused by ILO Convention No. 169 at the local level:

1. *The local construction of Indigenous and tribal identities,* especially the politics surrounding who should count as an Indigenous or tribal person, and how these ideas change and are institutionalized over time. There are at least two aspects to this. On the one hand, there are the subjective and micro-level dynamics whereby someone comes to think of themselves as Indigenous or tribal, and on the other, the way that the state formally classifies and counts its population.
2. *The historically specific features of the regnant citizenship regime,* including the rights and obligations to which citizens are entitled, with particular attention to whether Indigenous and tribal peoples can claim "special" rights, to land or otherwise.
3. *Land tenure regimes,* including land ownership patterns, the legal status of extractive industries, land use priorities, the existence of formally recognized communal land tenure options, and/or land tenure options specifically designed for recognizing Indigenous territories.

The logic is that investigating the interactions (or lack thereof) between these variables can help us better understand the material, socio-political, and ideological implications of Indigenous identity politics in relation to land struggles in different places in the twenty-first century. Importantly, national dynamics need to be thought of as embedded in a global political economy, pressured by the expansion of extractive industries, and influenced by an international human rights framework that calls for the protection of minority rights. By utilizing this analytical approach, we can go beyond decontextualized analyses that merely highlight differences between international law in theory and domestic policies in practice. The framework can be valuable beyond Mexico and even in contexts where ILO Convention 169 has not been ratified, insofar as segments of the population are mobilizing Indigenous identities and international law in the context of territorial disputes and anti-extractive struggles.

As was discussed throughout and in relation to the case of Mexico, the language in ILO Convention 169 is notoriously timid in relation to territorial struggles, arguably one of the most sensitive issues for Indigenous and tribal peoples globally. The Element drew attention to the limits of ILO Convention No. 169, *as it is written* as a tool to make claims to land. While the Convention acknowledges Indigenous and tribal peoples' right to self-determination, the fact that it does not grant them the right to veto concessions for extractive industries places serious limits on their ability to defend territory in the face of powerful economic interests. Relatedly, the framing of the Convention explicitly avoids confronting the state's claim over ownership of all subsoil resources, and merely stipulates that Indigenous communities are to be consulted over their exploitation. Even when the outcome of consultations is majority opposition to a particular type of land use, the result is not binding. The fundamental assumption underpinning the Convention's take on prior consultations is that consensus must be reached between parties. Ultimately, states reserve the rights to decide on the expansion of the extractive frontier, independent of the preferences of tribal and Indigenous peoples. Paradoxically, in practice, prior consultations have done more to legitimate the expansion of the extractive frontier than to limit its expansion insofar as they provide avenues to channel grievances and discontent. In short, the difficulty of confronting the power of extractive industries is not due to enforcement gaps nor the inappropriate application of the Convention, but rather a reflection of its reticence to challenge extractive industries, both public and private. The limits of the Convention in the context of land disputes are not merely a matter of a gap between international law in theory and domestic law in practice. Rather, they reflect the Convention's timid stance in relation to land conflicts, as well as its silences in relation to the power of global capital and its complicities with states.

A related and critically important implication of the way in which ILO Convention No. 169 has been adopted in Mexico and elsewhere is that critiques of the global political economic model, whose cumulative socio-environmental effects contribute directly to climate change and dispossession, are not at the center of the discussion. The focus on organizing prior consultations, particularly, has contributed to channeling discontent to the local level, as opposed to placing debates about national and international political economy center stage. Prior consultations create the veneer of some degree of democratic participation in processes that are generally vertically and undemocratically determined. The role and power of capital are removed from the equation, and disputes are to be sorted out on a case-by-case basis at the local level. This is not altogether surprising given that the ILO is premised on elaborating rules for making global capitalism work better, perhaps with somewhat less exploitation, via the creation and adoption of worker-friendly standards. The ILO is not in the business of questioning the economic model that creates conflicts over land in the first place.

Despite the limited material implications of ILO Convention 169 in the context of conflicts over territories claimed by Indigenous and tribal populations, its ideological and discursive reach has been noteworthy. The fact that the Convention espouses Indigenous peoples' right to their ancestral territories and their right to be consulted in all matters that may affect them encourages the mobilization of Indigeneity as part of conflicts over land and territory. We are living in a moment in which the centrality of Indigeneity as the basis on which land can be claimed is a particularly powerful frame, while other imaginable frames (arguments about having worked the land or being deserving of land due to poverty and landlessness, for instance) have less public visibility. Moreover, Convention 169 has been embraced by numerous Indigenous people and organizations worldwide as what they consider to be one of the few legal tools that can be mobilized to defend their rights and interests, however imperfectly. It has also directly influenced the content of regional human rights frameworks (notably that of the Inter-American Court of Human Rights, IACHR) as well as domestic politics in times of crisis (as in the context of the Zapatista uprising in Mexico and the peace negotiations in Guatemala). Even in countries where it has not been ratified, ILO Convention 169, alongside the posterior UN Declaration on the Rights of Indigenous Peoples and the strengthening of both national and transnational Indigenous and tribal peoples' rights movements, has positioned Indigeneity at the center of the global and domestic human rights agenda. These international norms have influenced discourses and frames of resistance to extractivism and land conflicts more generally. Consequently, contemporary critiques of the dominant development paradigm have become increasingly intertwined with Indigenous identity politics.

ILO Convention 169 can indeed be helpful as a legitimizing tool in the context of territorial disputes, but only domestic politics that are able to effectively challenge the power of extractive industries, agrarian elites, and the prioritization of large-scale infrastructure projects have successfully placed limits on these industries. Cases of the successful blocking of the expansion of extractivism and the defense of Indigenous territories have happened despite, rather than because of, the ratification of ILO Convention 169. In the face of inaction from the Mexican government, for example, the EZLN opted to take matters into their own hands. Instead of waiting for the state to grant them land rights and act on the numerous themes that are part of the San Andres Peace Accords, they decided to establish autonomous territories using force and grassroots power stemming from years of local organization. The EZLN was able to inspire global solidarity and raise substantial resources abroad in favor of building autonomous territories in the southern state of Chiapas. There are other examples from across the world in which people have managed to defend land from extractive industries, and these have not been the direct outcome of the domestic adoption of C169. Still, tracing the interrelationships between: (1) citizenship regimes, (2) land tenure regimes, and (3) Indigenous identity politics in particular times and places can provide a helpful analytical framework for understanding the extent to which Indigenous and tribal peoples rights may or may not be an effective framing in the context of land and anti-extractive struggles in specific places.

Disputes over land and extractivism are evidently not solely or even primarily about identity and cultural rights. They are also about unequal power relations, ecologically unequal exchange, the power of capital, and the prioritization of wealth accumulation to fuel the continued reproduction of the global capitalist economy. While ILO Convention No. 169 may prove useful as a legitimizing document to support claims to territories by people who have experienced various iterations of displacement and dispossession, it is crucial to keep in mind that effectively challenging extractive industries and guaranteeing a more equitable land distribution entails challenging our prevailing political economic logic and priorities, not solely the defense of the cultural rights of those that are able to mobilize Indigenous and tribal identities. The defense of Indigenous and tribal peoples' rights to land could therefore be one aspect of a wider political strategy seeking to transition to a world that places socio-economic justice and environmental stewardship at the core.

References

Anaya, James. 1996. *Indigenous Peoples in International Law*. Oxford: Oxford University Press.

Anaya, James. 2004. "International Human Rights and Indigenous Peoples: The Move toward the Multicultural State." *Arizona Journal of International and Comparative Law* 21(1): 13–61.

Assies, Willem. 2008. "Land Tenure and Tenure Regimes in Mexico: An Overview." *Journal of Agrarian Change* 8(1): 33–63.

Bebbington, Anthony and Jeffrey Bury (eds.). 2013. *Subterranean Struggles: New Dynamics of Mining, Oil, and Gas in Latin America*. Austin: University of Texas Press.

Borras, Jun, Jennifer Franco, Cristobal Kay and Max Spoor 2011. "Land Grabbing in Latin America and the Caribbean Viewed from Broader International Perspectives." Chile: FAO.

Borras, Jun, Jennifer Franco, Sergio Gómez, Cristobal Kay and Max Spoor. "Land Grabbing in Latin America and the Caribbean." *The Journal of Peasant Studies* 39: 845–72.

Bowen, John R. 2000. "Should We Have a Universal Concept of 'Indigenous Peoples' Rights?: Ethnicity and Essentialism in the Twenty-First Century." *Anthropology Today* 16(4): 12–16.

Bridge, Gavin. 2004. "Mapping the Bonanza: Geographies of Mining Investment in an Era of Neoliberal Reform." *Professional Geographer* 56(3): 406–21.

Burchardt, Hans-Jürgen and Kristina Dietz. 2014. "(Neo-)Extractivism – a New Challenge for Development Theory from Latin America." *Third World Quarterly* 35(3): 468–86.

Castellanos, Laura. 2018. "Estos 108 mexicanos fueron asesinados por defender nuestros bosques y ríos." Remamx.org. December 5.

Castree, Noel. 2004. "Differential Geographies: Place, Indigenous Rights and 'local' Resources." *Political Geography* 23(2): 133–67.

CEACR Direct Requests. 1993, 1998, 2001, 2011, 2019. Geneva: International Labor Organization.

CEACR Observations. 1998, 2005, 2007, 2008, 2019. Geneva: International Labor Organization.

Champagne, Duane. 2013. "UNDRIP (United Nations Declaration on the Rights of Indigenous Peoples): Human, Civil and Indigenous Rights." *Wicazo Sa Review* 28(1): 9–22.

Chase, Veronika M. 2019. "The Changing Face of Environmental Governance in the Brazilian Amazon: Indigenous and Traditional Peoples Promoting Norm Diffusion." *Revista Brasileira de Política Internacional* 62(2). https://doi.org/10.1590/0034-7329201900208.

CIDH. 2016. "Resolución 51/2016. Medida cautelar no. 60-14. Ampliación de beneficiarios a favor de integrantes de la Comunidad Indígena de Choréachi respecto de México." OAS. October 26, 2016.

Dunlap, Alexander. 2018. "'A Bureaucratic Trap:' Free, Prior and Informed Consent (FPIC) and Wind Energy Development in Juchitán, Mexico." *Capitalism Nature Socialism* 29(4): 88–108.

Flores, Nancy. 2018. "La minería causa más de 15.000 conflictos sociales en México." RT. February 27.

Fontana, Lorenza and Jean Grugel. 2016. "The Politics of Indigenous Participation Through 'Free Prior Informed Consent': Reflections from the Bolivian Case." *World Development* 77: 249–61.

Galinier, Jacques and Antoinette Molinié. 2013. *The Neo-Indians: A Religion for the Third Millenium*. Denver: University Press of Colorado.

Global Witness. 2022. "Decade of Defiance: Ten Years of Reporting Land and Environmental Activism Worldwide." London.

Gómez Rivera, Magdalena. 2013. "Los Pueblos Indígenas y La Razón de Estado En México: Elementos Para Un Balance." *Nueva Antropología* 26(78): 43–62.

González Oropeza, Manuel. 2005. "Aplicación Del Convenio 169 de La OIT En México." In David Cienfuegos Salgado, Miguel Alejandro López Olvera, eds., *Estudios En Homenaje a Don Jorge Fernández Ruiz: Derecho Constitucional y Política*, Mexico City: UNAM, 255–67.

Gudynas, Eduardo. 2015. *Extractivismos: Ecología, economía y política de un modo de entender el desarrollo y la naturaleza*. Cochabamba: CEDIB.

Gudynas, Eduardo. 2016. "Teología de Los Extractivismos." *Tabula Rasa* 24: 11–23.

Hale, Charles. 2002. "Does Multiculturalism Menace? Governance, Cultural Rights and the Politics of Identity in Guatemala." *Journal of Latin American Studies* 34(3): 485–524.

Haley, Brian. 2024. "In Cahoots with Neo-Indigenism." *Genealogy* 8(99): 1–14.

Haley, Brian and Larry Wilcoxon. 2005. "How Spaniards Became Chumash and other Tales of Ethnogenesis." *American Anthropologist* 107(3): 432–45.

Harvey, David. 2005. *A Brief History of Neoliberalism*. New York: Oxford University Press.

Hays, Jennifer and Jakob Kronik. 2020. "The ILO PRO169 Programme: Learning from Technical Cooperation in Latin America and South Africa." *International Journal of Human Rights* 24(2–3): 191–213.

Hodgson, Dorothy. 2002. "Introduction: Comparative Perspectives on the Indigenous Rights Movement in Africa and the Americas." *American Anthropologist* 104(4), 1037-1049.

ILO. 1989. *Indigenous and Tribal Peoples Convention No. 169*. Geneva: International Labor Organization.

ILO. 2009. *Indigenous and Tribal Peoples' Rights in Practice: A Guide to ILO Convention No. 169*. Geneva: International Labor Organization.

ILO. 2013. *Understanding the Indigenous and Tribal Peoples Convention, 1989 (No. 169)*. Geneva: International Labor Organization.

ILO. 2019. *Implementing the ILO Indigenous and Tribal Peoples Convention No. 169: Towards an inclusive, sustainable and just future*. Geneva: International Labor Organization.

IWGIA. 2018. "Outcome Document: Defending the Defenders." (September): 1–8.

Klare, Michael. 2012. *The Race for What's Left: The Global Scramble for the World's Last Resources*. New York: Metropolitan Books.

Larsen, Peter. 2020. "Contextualising Ratification and Implementation: A Critical Appraisal of ILO Convention 169 from a Social Justice Perspective." *International Journal of Human Rights* 24(2–3): 94–111.

Larsen, Peter Bille and Jérémie Gilbert. 2020. "Indigenous Rights and ILO Convention 169: Learning from the Past and Challenging the Future." *International Journal of Human Rights* 24(2–3): 83–93.

Larsen, Peter and Louise Nolle. 2020. "Enabling Human Rights-Based Development for Indigenous and Tribal Peoples? Summarising the 25th Anniversary Global Policy Debate on ILO Convention 169." *International Journal of Human Rights* 24(2–3): 279–92.

Leal, Pablo. 2007. "Participation: The Ascendancy of a Buzzword in the Neo-Liberal Era." *Development in Practice* 17(4–5): 539–48.

Lemus, Jesús. 2018. *México a cielo abierto: De cómo el boom minero resquebrajó al país*. Mexico City: Grijalbo.

Leroux, Darryl. 2019. *Distorted Descent: White Claims to Indigenous Identity*. Winnipeg: University of Manitoba Press.

Leroux, Darryl. 2024. "Proximity, Family Lore, and False Claims to an Algonquin Identity." *Genealogy* 8(125): 1–23.

Ley de Hidrocarburos. 2014. "Decreto por el que se expide la Ley de Hidrocarburos y se reforman diversas disposiciones de la Ley de Inversión

Extranjera; Ley Minera, y Ley de Asociaciones Público Privadas." *Diario Oficial de la Federación*. August 11.

Ley, Sandra, Shannan Mattiace and Guillermo Trejo . 2019. "Indigenous Resistance to Criminal Governance: Why Regional Ethnic Autonomy Institutions Protect Communities from Narco Rule in Mexico." *Latin American Research Review* 54(1): 181–200.

Li, Tania. 2010. "Indigeneity, Capitalism and the Management of Dispossession." *Current Anthropology* 51(3): 385–414.

López Portillo, José. 1977. "Iniciativa de Reformas a los artículos 7° y 10 de la Ley Reglamentaria del Artículo 27 Constitucional en el Ramo del Petróleo, enviada por el Ejecutivo de la Unión." Mexico City.

Loveman, Mara. 2014. *National Colors: Racial Classification and the State in Latin America*. Oxford: Oxford University Press.

Marshall, Thomas Humphrey and Tom Bottomore. 1987. *Citizenship and Social Class*. London: Pluto Press.

Navarro-López, América. 2024. "Fifty Years of Forced Displacement in Chiapas, Mexico: From Political Conflicts to Cartel Conflicts." *Journal of Latin American Geography* 23(2): 91–131.

Peet, Richard and Michael Watts. 2004. *Liberation Ecologies: Environment, Development and Social Movements*. London: Routledge.

Perreault, Tom. 2015. "Performing Participation: Mining, Power, and the Limits of Public Consultation in Bolivia." *Journal of Latin American and Caribbean Anthropology* 20(3): 433–51.

Pimentel, Spensky. 2021. "The Right to Say No: Extractivism and Territorial Struggles." *Revista Ambiente e Sociedade* 24. https://doi.org/10.1590/1809-4422asoc20210159vu2021L5NR.

Pirsoul, Nicolas. 2019. "The Deliberative Deficit of Prior Consultation Mechanisms." *Australian Journal of Political Science* 54(2): 255–71.

Riofrancos, Thea. 2020. *Resource Radicals: From Petro-Nationalism to Post-Extractivism in Ecuador*. Durham: Duke University Press.

Robles Berlanga, Héctor, 2000. "Propiedad de la tierra y población indígena." *Estudios Agrarios* 14: 123–47.

Rodríguez Piñero, Luis. 2005. *Indigenous Peoples, Postcolonialism and International Law*. Oxford: Oxford University Press.

San Andrés Accords. 1996. Mexico.

Santaolalla, Ximena. 2023. "State Crime, Extraction and Cartels: The Meaning of Mining in Guerrero, Mexico." *ReVista: Harvard Review of Latin America*.

Sassen, Saskia. 2006. *Territory, Authority, Rights: From Medieval to Global Assemblages*. New York: Princeton University Press.

Sassen, Saskia. 2013. "Land Grabs Today: Feeding the Disassembling of National Territory." *Globalizations* 10(1): 25–46.

Sener. 2018. "Consultas Previas, Libres e Informadas a Comunidades y Pueblos Indígenas en el Sector Energético." June 1. Mexico City: Secretaría de Energía.

Shah, Alpa. 2007. "The Dark Side of Indigeneity?: Indigenous People, Rights and Development in India." *History Compass* 5(6): 1806–32.

Speed, Shannon and Maria Teresa Sierra. 2005. "Critical Perspectives on Human Rights and Multiculturalism in Neoliberal Latin America." *PoLAR: Political and Legal Anthropology Review* 28(1): 1–9.

Stamatopoulous, Elsa. 1994. "Indigenous Peoples and the United Nations: Human Rights as a Developing Dynamic." *Human Rights Quarterly* 16(1): 58–81.

Stern, Steve and Scott Straus (eds.). 2014. *The Human Rights Paradox: Universality and Its Discontents*. Madison: University of Wisconsin Press.

Svampa, Maristella. 2015. "Commodities Consensus: Neoextractivism and Enclosure of the Commons in Latin America." *South Atlantic Quarterly* 114(1): 65–82.

Swepston, Lee. 2020. "Progress through Supervision of Convention No. 169." *International Journal of Human Rights* 24(2–3): 112–26.

Temper, Leah, Daniela del Bene, and Joan Martinez-Alier. 2015. "Mapping the Frontiers and Front Lines of Global Environmental Justice: The EJAtlas." *Journal of Political Ecology* 22: 254–78.

Veltmeyer, Henry and James Petras (eds.). 2014. *New Extractivism: A Post-Neoliberal Development Model or Imperialism of the Twenty-First Century?* New York: Zed Books.

Yashar, Deborah. 1999. "Democracy, Indigenous Movements, and the Postliberal Challenge in Latin America." *World Politics* 52(1): 76–104.

Yashar, Deborah. 2005. *Citizenship in Latin America: The Rise of Indigenous Movements and the Postliberal Challenge*. Cambridge: Cambridge University Press.

Yashar, Deborah J. 2007. "Resistance and Identity Politics in an Age of Globalization." *Annals of the American Academy of Political and Social Science* 610(1): 160–81.

Zoomers, Annelies. 2010. "Globalisation and the Foreignisation of Space: Seven Processes Driving the Current Global Land Grab." *The Journal of Peasant Studies* 37(2): 429–47.

Research Ethics Statement

Ethical approval for this research was obtained from the University of Wisconsin Education and Social/Behavioral Science Institutional Review Board (study number 2018-1488). Written and verbal informed consent was obtained from Lourdes Melgar Palacios, interviewed as part of this study.

Cambridge Elements

Indigenous Environmental Research

Series Editors
Dina Gilio-Whitaker
California State University San Marcos

Dina Gilio-Whitaker (Colville Confederated Tribes) is a lecturer of American Indian Studies at California State University San Marcos, and an independent educator in American Indian environmental policy and other issues. She teaches courses on environmentalism and American Indians, traditional ecological knowledge, religion and philosophy, Native women's activism, American Indians and sports, and decolonization. Dina is the award-winning *As Long as Grass Grows: The Indigenous Fight for Environmental Justice* (Beacon Press, 2019). She is also an award-winning journalist, with her work appearing in *Indian Country Today*, the *Los Angeles Times*, Time.com, *The Boston Globe*, and many more.

Clint R. Carroll
University of Colorado Boulder

Clint Carroll is an Associate Professor in the Department of Ethnic Studies at the University of Colorado Boulder. A citizen of the Cherokee Nation, he works at the intersections of Indigenous studies, anthropology, and political ecology. His first book, *Roots of Our Renewal: Ethnobotany and Cherokee Environmental Governance* (University of Minnesota Press, 2015), explores how tribal natural resource managers navigate the material and structural conditions of settler colonialism, and how recent efforts in cultural revitalization inform such practices through traditional Cherokee governance and local environmental knowledge. He is an active member of the Native American and Indigenous Studies Association and the Society for Applied Anthropology. He also serves on the editorial boards for *Cultural Anthropology* and *Environment and Society*.

Joy Porter
University of Birmingham

Joy Porter is University of Birmingham 125th Anniversary Chair, Professor of Indigenous and Environmental History and Principal Investigator of the Treatied Spaces Research Group. She is the Principal Investigator for "Brightening the Covenant Chain: Revealing Cultures of Diplomacy Between the Iroquois and the British Crown" (2021–2025) and "Historic Houses Global Connections: Revisioning Two Northern Ireland Historic Houses and Estates" (2024–2027). Joy has over 65 publications, including four research monographs and three other books. She received the Wordcraft Circle of Native Writers Writer of the Year Award for *The Cambridge Companion to Native American Literature* (Cambridge University Press, 2005) and a Choice Outstanding Academic Title Award for *To be Indian: The Life of Iroquois-Seneca Arthur Caswell Parker* (Oklahoma, 2023, 2001). Her latest book is *Trauma, Primitivism and the First World War: The Making of Frank Prewett* (Bloomsbury, 2021). She was born in Derry, in the North of Ireland.

Associate Editor
Matthias Wong
National University of Singapore

Matthias Wong is Senior Tutor at the National University of Singapore and an Associate of the Treatied Spaces Research Group at the University of Birmingham. His research is in the environmental humanities, specifically in the use of digital methods to recover Indigenous presence in historical sources such as maps and treaties, and in reconnecting Indigenous collections in museums with their source communities. He co-leads the "Green Toolkit for a New Space Economy" project, which aims to widen the space sector's understanding of sustainability to include the cultural and social dimensions. His collaborators include King's Digital Lab at King's College London, The Alan Turing Institute, and Nordamerika Native Museum Zurich. His research interests are on the process of meaning-making, particularly in understanding senses of time and place, and on the repercussions of trauma and disruption. His research on early modern futurity has been published in *Historical Research*, and he teaches courses on cultural astronomy, public history, and digital history.

Advisory Board

Ann McGrath, *Australian National University*
Camilla Brattland, *Arctic University of Norway (UIT)*
Dalo Njera, *Mzuzu University*
Kalpana Giri, *The Regional Community Forestry Training Center for Asia and the Pacific (RECOFTC)*
Simone Athayde, *Florida International University*
Joe Bryan, *University of Colorado Boulder*
Kanyinke Sena, *Egerton University*
Kyle Powys Whyte, *University of Michigan*
Dale Turner, *University of Toronto*
Michael Hathaway, *Simon Fraser University*
Paige West, *Columbia University*
Pratik Chakrabarti, *University of Houston*
Rauna Kuokkanen, *University of Lapland*
Shannon Speed, *University of California Los Angeles*
Mike Dockry, *University of Minnesota*

About the Series

Elements in Indigenous Environmental Research offers state-of-the-art interdisciplinary analyses within the rapidly growing area of Indigenous environmental research. The series investigates how environmental issues and processes relate to Indigenous socio-economic, cultural and political dynamics.

Cambridge Elements⁼

Indigenous Environmental Research

Elements in the Series

Defending Community, Territory, and Indigenous Environmental Relations
Levi Gahman, Filiberto Penados, Cristina Coc and Shelda-Jane Smith

"Alaska" Is Not a Blank Space: Unsettling Aldo Leopold's Odyssey
Julianne Warren

Indigenous Rights to Land Versus Extractivism: The Promise and Limits of ILO Convention No. 169 in Mexico
Tamara A. Wattnem

A full series listing is available at: www.cambridge.org/EIER

For EU product safety concerns, contact us at Calle de José Abascal, 56-1°,
28003 Madrid, Spain or eugpsr@cambridge.org.

www.ingramcontent.com/pod-product-compliance
Lightning Source LLC
LaVergne TN
LVHW021736060526
838200LV00052B/3306